also by Gene and Judith Tate O'Brien
published by Paulist Press

**A Redeeming State: A Handbook
for Couples Planning Remarriage
in the Church**

**A Redeeming State: Leader's Guide
for Couples Planning Remarriage
in the Church**

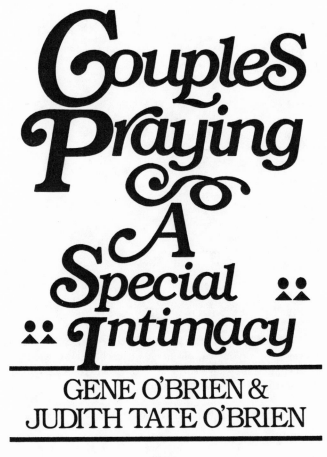

Couples Praying
A Special Intimacy

GENE O'BRIEN &
JUDITH TATE O'BRIEN

Paulist Press
New York/Mahwah

Library of Congress Cataloging-in-Publication Data

O'Brien, Gene.
    Couples praying.

    1. Married people—Religious life. 2. Prayer.
I. O'Brien, Judith Tate. II. Title.
BV4596.M3037   1986   248.3′2′0880655   86-91497
ISBN 0-8091-2816-0 (pbk.)

Published by Paulist Press
997 Macarthur Boulevard
Mahwah, New Jersey 07430

Printed and bound in the United States of America

Contents

Introduction

Big Vic Galier, breathing with cancerous lungs, lives on borrowed time.

When doctors told Vic he had only a few months to live, he experienced a sharp turn in the road of his life. It was as if he had been traveling north, and the road suddenly swerved to the west. He journeyed on that new road with fear, fury, hope, and occasional peace. It's a journey most people make alone. But Vic had a companion.

Rita Galier, traveled beside her husband with an uncommon closeness. A 26-year habit of praying together made that level of intimacy possible.

For Vic and Rita and for many other couples, couple prayer provides a richness in marriage not found in other ways. We hope this book will help more couples discover or rediscover that richness.

Once we attended a two-day workshop on prayer, and when we finished we were too scared to pray! We had learned that prayer is complicated indeed. There were certain steps we needed to follow if we were going to pray "right." We felt paralyzed by our awareness of how many ways we could foul up. It was embarrassing enough to try to pray "right" in private, and we weren't about to display our ignorance before each other by trying it jointly! That workshop stopped us dead in our tracks for a while.

Because of that workshop experience, we hesitated when editor Doug Fisher suggested we write a book on couple prayer.

1

How could we encourage couples to pray together without guilting them if they don't? How could we show some how-to's without confusing them? How could we make the book theologically sound without making it pedantic and preachy?

We finally hit upon an approach that pleases us. We hope it will please the reader as much.

In Part One of the book, six couples share their experiences of praying together. Like love-making, couple prayer varies with each couple. There are no hard and fast rules.

Certainly the couples in these interviews make significant theological points, but they make those points in familial language that seems to us very refreshing. It's what one couple called "kitchen theology"—not that it isn't sound theology but that it is suited in language and emphasis to couples in their homes.

In short, the six couples who share their prayer experiences in Part One of this book show how couple prayer can lead ordinary couples to extraordinary depths of marriage and to a distinctive awareness of God's presence with them in their cars and kitchens and bedrooms.

In Part Two of the book, we lift up some typical marriage and family events and reflect on them through Scripture.

Although each marriage is unique, most marriages share similar happenings. Most couples wash dishes, pay bills, make love, and worry about the kids. Two couples could share these same four events in the same day and end up in two entirely different places—one couple unified and one couple in tension.

What makes marriages unique is not different experiences but different attitudes about similar experiences.

The reflections in this part of the book deal with changing attitudes (conversion) and sharing and honoring each other's uniqueness (unity).

In Part Two, we emphasize dialogical prayer.

When our prayer is a monologue, we send messages to God in a one-way stream of words. When our prayer is a dialogue, on the other hand, we first let God speak while we listen. Then we respond. Dialogical prayer changes us, because we are changed by what we hear—*really* hear—and understand.

We believe it is possible, even simple, for couples to enrich themselves through prayer together.

This book is for all Christian couples. For those who already pray together, the book may serve as a renewal. For those who would like to pray together but for some reason haven't, the book may be an incentive to begin. For those who have never thought of praying together, the book may open up a new possibility.

Part One

Stories About Couples
Who Pray Together:
A Special Intimacy

Since example can be both an effective teacher and an inspiring model, it seems more appropriate to present some examples of couple prayer than to outline a system of prayer.

Many couples pray together. In this book, six of them, representing ninety-six years of marriage and sixty-one years of couple prayer, tell their own stories about how they pray together and what praying together means to them. Parts of their stories are funny and parts sad. All of them are moving.

No significant scientific studies have been made of couples who pray together, but it seems quite probable that those who share their experiences here are representative of most couples who do.

Important themes that clearly emerge from the six stories that follow can be clustered under three headings: (1) commitment, (2) closeness, and (3) conversion.

Commitment

"We've flowed with it through some dry periods and some good periods, but we've never given up on it," says David Best. *"We don't keep driving at it, saying 'It's gotta have this or that format.' For us, the issue is simply to pray. To talk. To talk and pray. To do those two things together."*

David is talking about commitment.

Commitment gives shape and depth to important human endeavors. Marriage without commitment would be shapeless and shallow. The same is true of ministry, career, the practice of faith, effective parenting—and prayer. These situations sometimes carry peak moments or even abiding satisfaction, but at least occasionally they also produce rough times and dry periods.

Those are the times commitment can carry people to the other side of the storm.

When couples are committed to couple prayer, they may skip a day or two once in a while because of anger, sickness, or other disabilities; but they know they will resume praying together. Couple prayer is not something they do in crisis. It's something they do in good times and in bad.

Commitments are easier to make and to keep when others give support and example.

Retorno, a Scripture-based couple prayer program, inspires couples to make a commitment precisely because it does provide example and a sense of community.

Couples who make a commitment to pray together but who do not experience community express a yearning to be in touch with other couples who have similar ideals.

"A big part of our prayer is our plea for some experience of community, some sense of support that a parish can't seem to offer," says Lisa White Smith. *"We seldom feel any kind of oneness with other lay persons—married couples who experience life in a way similar to the way we do."*

Joyce Russell echoes that longing. *"I need support from other couples who pray together. I'd like to hear them talk about how they pray, about the benefits and difficulties. It would help me to know we're not doing something odd!"*

Although the act of praying alone with one's spouse is private and intimate, praying couples nevertheless either do experience or want to experience knowing other couples who also pray together.

That kind of support and example would certainly make commitment easier.

Closeness

"When you pray with someone, you get down to where they really live inside themselves," explains Bob Calibani. *"And you let them into that place inside yourself."*

Without any jargon, Bob is speaking of the great mystery of intimacy.

God's plan for marriage is that couples be unified, that they become "one flesh." "One flesh" does not mean that couples become fused in such a way that they lose their own identities. It means that they become intimate in such a way that they clarify their identities by mutual and loving revelation. Unity, then, means loving intimacy.

It would be inaccurate to say married couples either experience intimacy or don't. It is more accurate to say they experience less intimacy or more. It's a matter of degree.

Language, one of the most distinctive characteristics that makes humans different from other creatures, is a means of intimacy. Language can reveal little or much and greatly determines whether couples are on the high end or the low end of the intimacy continuum.

Language used in prayer—when prayer is really honest—tends to reveal much. Possibly people are never so self-revealing as they are in authentic prayer. God reads hearts. Pretense is out of the question. So in prayer, people reveal who they really are. They also reveal who God is to them.

When people reveal what is inside themselves—memories, aspirations, emotions—they understand themselves better. For to reveal is to make more clear. Thus, people experience their own feelings more clearly when they put words around those feelings. Otherwise, however strong the emotions may be, they remain shadowy and undefined.

In prayer, then, people can learn more clearly who they are.

When couples stand *together* before God in this kind of prayer, they can also experience each other more deeply. In this way, couple prayer deepens marriage unity.

Another way couple prayer deepens marriage unity is by hastening reconciliation. All the couples interviewed in this book talk about the relation of prayer to reconciliation.

"We often end those times of separation through prayer," Rita Galier says. *"If Vic has been mad at me, for example, he might get up one morning and say, 'Let's pray this morning.' That's the start. It never fails—it never fails—that reconciliation takes place."*

Probably the very simple act of touching during prayer also hastens reconciliation. Most of the couples mentioned that they physically touch each other when they pray.

Linda Baustert describes it this way: *"Part of the healing, I think, comes from touch. Don and I sit next to each other on the couch, so we're touching. When we pray, we always touch. That's our signal. We'll either hold hands or something. You can't stay mad when you're touching like that."*

Reconciliation in marriage is essential for intimacy.

When people are hurt or angry, they usually become defensive. Blaming is a common defense. Withdrawal is another. Defenses distance people. They are behaviors that either push away or pull back. So when couples quarrel frequently or keep up their defenses over long periods of time, they are not likely to be close.

In prayer together, couples are more apt to let down their defenses.

This doesn't mean that praying couples don't experience disagreements, become angry, and throw up defenses. It means that they are less likely to let anger fester. It means that the "climate" of their relationship is one of peace.

Conversion

"Words without action—that's not prayer to my way of thinking," says Don Baustert. *"I can pray for someone who is sick or lonely, but if I don't get off my butt and go visit them, those words are meaningless."*

Prayer can become a powerful conversion experience.

It's true that people reveal themselves to God in prayer. What is even more basic is that God reveals God.

God reveals himself in his Word. For this reason, personal prayer as well as liturgical worship needs to be informed (formed from within) by Scripture.

Praying people, listening to hear God's Word, gradually learn more and more about God.

Then praying people do what they hear. They let themselves be changed by God's Word. Therein lies conversion.

As long as people live, they are "on the way"—on the way in their one and only journey of life. Every time people turn a little more Godward on this journey, they experience conversion. *Conversion* means *turning*. People on the way make many turns. Many of those turns may be toward God.

The test of true prayer lies in the answer to these two questions: Do we *hear* God's Word? Do we *do* God's Word?

Sometimes the doing (conversion) is related to personal habits.

"For me, prayer is an act of honesty," says David Best. *"I have to face, for example, the truth that, despite my mask of being in control, I'm not a confrontive person and that sometimes I'm untruthful by not being straightforward. Once*

I say that out loud to Jane and God, I have to do something about it. I have to make at least a little bitty change. I guess that's called conversion."

Sometimes people do God's Word by becoming more committed to their marriages.

"We've been more supportive of one another in the past few months than ever before," admits Joyce Russell. *"It goes along with my sense that—for the first time, really—I am committed to our marriage—and with my awareness that I was holding back during the first eight years."*

Other times God calls people to do his Word in other ways: by altering their life style, by becoming more involved in working for peace in the world, by being more generous in ministering to others.

The point is this: authentic prayer changes people.

When couples pray together, they can help one another hear God's Word more clearly. They can also support one another in doing God's Word.

Jackie Calibani sums up the process this way:

"Praying together is a little like having a three-way conversation. We confide in one another and in God. We attend to one another and to God."

What a powerful intimacy such prayer could bring in a marriage! And what conversion!

"I Don't Like To Not Pray"

> *"The only time I feel awkward praying with David is when I'm not feeling good about myself or when there's tension between us. I hate to pray at those times because I know I'm going to have to be honest and then I'll be vulnerable and probably have to make some change. But we usually end up praying anyway, because, no matter what, I don't like to not pray."* Jane Best

David and Jane Best probably come as close as any couple to fitting that figment of the national imagination referred to as the typical American couple. When Phillips Petroleum Company, wanting to test a new street surfacing material, looked for a street in a typical middle-class mid-America neighborhood, they chose Somerset, the street where David and Jane live.

David, 43, blond, athletic, and sensitive, owns a construction business. Jane, 42, fair-skinned and red-haired, works part-time in David's office and is straightforward about her preference for homemaking. They were high school sweethearts, have been married 23 years, and have three children.

Beneath all these typical-seeming appearances, David and Jane have found depths of joy and intimacy that seem rare in modern marriage. These good gifts didn't just happen; the Bests worked for them. Couple prayer is their wellspring.

DAVID: I'm trying to remember if we prayed together before Retorno. Yeah, we did some. When we worked on the

13

Marriage Encounter team, before we'd go in to start a weekend, we'd almost always sit in the car and hold hands and ask God to be with us and with the couples who'd be there. But we hadn't made a commitment to pray together until Retorno. That was in 1975. Ever since then, we've prayed almost daily.

At first we tried at night because we just knew I could never get up in the morning. We had a knock-down-drag-out over that. I bet God got a chuckle over that—a couple fighting about when they'd pray! I thought, "No one's going to get me up at six in the morning." I'm not a morning person. But it got impossible to pray at night. The phone would ring. Jane would fall asleep. (She's not a night person.) The kids would come in. So early on, we decided morning was the only way to go. We get up about an hour earlier than we used to. It's just part of our routine now. We get a cup of coffee, sit down, talk a little bit, and end with a prayer.

JANE: I'll bring his coffee in—we pray in the bedroom—and say, "David, coffee's here." That's how we begin. We never start with a formal prayer, but in our mind, that entire morning conversation—starting with the coffee—is part of our prayer together. We talk about whatever's going on with us. Then we hold hands. That's our signal to close our conversation by lifting it up in a more formal way to the Father.

A lot of times, our prayer seems really repetitious. But I've come to realize that our lives *are* repetitious. I bet if the four of us went into separate rooms and made out a list of what has concerned us the past week, there wouldn't be half a dozen things that wouldn't be on everybody's list. Work. Kids. Bills. Relationships. So when we talk with God, we find ourselves talking about the same things over and over. That's okay. You can't have a big drama in your life every week just to keep God interested.

Take the kids. You have them, and then you've got them for at least 18 years. We pray for our kids every day. God probably gets tired of hearing it. "Look out after them, Father. They're yours." I really do believe they're God's. It's reassuring to me to pray for the kids. It's sort of like worrying can be put aside. It doesn't mean nothing will go wrong, but Somebody is helping them—and us—through whatever happens.

Or take David's work. Our conversation-prayer includes a way of listening to God, talking over hard decisions with the definite attempt to do what God wants us to do as his adult son and daughter—like the time David had to deal with "James," an employee with a drug problem. Or the time he had to fire "Tom." Or the times he has to choose between being honest or losing a bid.

DAVID: Yeah, and talking things over like that with each other and with our God keeps us honest and it sort of forces us to do the hard thing that's right instead of the easy thing—at least sometimes.

Probably the reason prayer works for us is that we haven't put a lot of expectations or rules on ourselves. We've flowed with it through some dry periods and some good periods, but we've never given up on it. Whatever it is, it is. We don't keep driving at it, saying, "It's gotta have this or that format." For us, the issue is simply to pray. To talk. To talk and pray. To do those two things together.

I don't think the Church has a realistic spirituality for couples. We just can't operate out of a structure that fits monks or mystics. In my observation, that structure doesn't even work for most priests. But yet couples keep trying to imitate that model or to judge their spirituality by that model. It just doesn't work. We need a model of spirituality that fits marriage, and I think that'll have to come from couples. So right now, we're still struggling.

JANE: I agree with what David said. We've been really fortunate, I think, because some very special people in the Church have helped us understand the holiness of the *daili-*

ness of marriage. But we didn't learn that from the pulpit. I don't think the teaching Church really teaches this to couples. It isn't made clear enough—that just regular marriage is sacramental, that listening to one another, cooking, going to work—it's all sacred. I really believe that. I just wouldn't put anything before that.

I think couples are beginning to discover their own sacramentality. Marriage Encounter and Retorno help a lot, especially for those who stay involved for a while. The Renew program helps, too. But still I wish we had more help from the teaching Church. Maybe it's been there and I just haven't heard it. Praying together helps us keep this teaching in our minds.

I used to turn to God just as a problem-solver. I went to church and sang and all, but with one side of my mind I'd be busy planning a menu or making a dress. Unless I had a problem. Then I prayed! Praying with David daily helps me keep aware that God is with us all the time. All I have to do is invite him in. Golly, to have a neat gift like that and not to take five minutes to connect with him, to ask him in! I get really angry with myself when I don't do it.

I can still have crummy days, and lots of times I act really un-Christian, but God's right there to give me a little nudge, to love me anyway.

DAVID: Another thing about our couple prayer is I definitely know Jane better—and probably know myself better, too. It's not something that I can say, "Oh, yeah, I know this about her and I wouldn't know it if we hadn't been praying all these years." It's more like walking with her in a special close way for years. Kind of seeing what she sees and knowing what she feels and thinks.

There's a real comfortableness in it. I think I can tell her anything. And when I tell her—and God—that's often when I learn those things about myself.

For example, sometimes I still feel far away from God. It's a feeling I've had off and on all my life. The difference now is that I can say, "I don't feel close to you, God," or "I've been drinking too much or not doing this or that and that makes me feel estranged from you." It used to be I'd just not say anything *to* God or *about* him. It's hard for me now to remember how that was.

For me, prayer is an act of honesty. I have to face, for example, the truth that, despite my mask of being in control, I'm not a confrontive person and that sometimes I'm untruthful by not being straightforward. Once I say that out loud to Jane and God, I have to do something about it. I have to make at least a little bitty change. I guess that's called conversion.

JANE: David had always appeared to be in control. Now that we pray together, I know the David that lives down underneath all that control. I hear his needs, his fears, his calls for help. And I love him more than I ever loved the David who always seemed so in control.

He might pray and I'll think, "Golly, I didn't really realize how he's feeling about that." Maybe he said it when we were talking, but then I hear him say it to God and think, "I didn't really listen to him a while ago."

Prayer keeps us honest with each other. You just can't sit there and pray together with God if you haven't come clean with each other.

We've had many tears when we've been angry and pray into reconciliation. But we just don't go to sleep angry anymore. We might go to bed, but we don't go to sleep because we've been snarling and ugly with each other. So we lay there and toss and finally decide that, since it's going on four o'clock, we'd better get down to the business at hand. That seems to happen about twice a year and it's awful. Around four o'clock, we get up and make up. Inevitably, we end that with a prayer.

It's scary to remember that the first ten years of our marriage held so much anger and so little reconciliation.

Praying together has probably deepened our sexual love, too, because, well if you bare your soul, you're just more open with one another. We're more relaxed in sex. We've learned to accept the human side, to take advantage of the moment. You can't just wait (the way we used to try to do) till the moment is wrapped up in white paper and blue ribbon. Same way in prayer. We take what we have—even when it's less than ideal. Sometimes we have a Bible or a nice book or a beautiful insight—and sometimes we just have two minutes! Like once in a while, David will say, "I don't have time to sit down, but come here"; and he'll hold me in his arms and we might say a quick prayer standing there. I like that. Even if it's just fifteen seconds. It's real.

"It Doesn't Work
If You Aren't Touching"

*"We pray in bed. We usually hold hands. Sometimes if
we're real tired, one of us will just slide a leg over to make
physical contact. We have to be touching when we pray.
It doesn't work if you aren't touching."* Jackie Calibani

Bob and Jackie Calibani have been married eleven years.
Between them, they have five children.

Dark-eyed Bob, hailing from the east coast, describes
himself as "strictly a tomato-sauce Italian." Bob is emotional,
voluble, and devoted to his family.

Slower-talking blue-eyed Jackie seems to be one of those
super women who balances her jobs at home with those at her
office with nary a misstep.

The Calibanis have met the challenge of forming a step-
family the same way they have met other challenges: not without struggles but overall with gentle wit and deep faith.

JACKIE: We've been married eleven years. We've
prayed together ten years. We pray every night. Well, almost
every night. We've skipped a few or abbreviated a few because
I've fallen asleep.

I can't remember the very first time we prayed together,
but I know it was hard. It was kind of embarrassing at first.
Prayer has always been very private for me. It's one thing to
pray in a group—which Bob and I had done in charismatic

prayer groups. But it's another thing to pray just with your husband. There's more of an exposure of things deep in your mind.

We don't have a formula. It's just talking, the way we're talking right now. If there were rules to follow, I probably wouldn't do it. Rules make me nervous. I probably wouldn't want to expose my ignorance.

Praying together is a little like having a three-way conversation. We confide in one another and in God. We attend to one another and to God. Sometimes Bob will pray about something that he and I haven't even talked about. At those times, I feel kind of as though I'm eavesdropping. But it's okay because they both—God and Bob—know I'm listening in!

We each read the Bible a lot. We don't read it together much, but we'll talk about it. When we drive in to work, we talk a lot. And sometimes when something in the Bible or in another book strikes us, we'll read it to each other. I suppose that's all part of our prayer together, but our actual prayer in bed is more related to our daily lives. The kids. Our relationship. Our parents. Our jobs.

BOB: We began couple prayer shortly after getting involved in the charismatic movement. That's probably why we nearly always start with the words, "Praise you, Jesus" or "Glory and praise to you, Father." From there we give thanks.

One thing the charismatic movement did for me was help me become more aware of God's tremendous goodness, his love. It's just overwhelming. Lots of times, our prayer consists totally of thanksgiving and praise.

Even I—and I'm not a guy that's easily embarrassed—I found it a risk at first to pray with Jackie. I can't remember how long it took to get used to it. Not very long, though. A week, maybe. For Jackie, it may have taken a little longer. Now it's very safe, very comfortable.

As Jackie said, we don't burden ourselves with a lot of rules. I have just one rule: KISS. "Keep It Simple, Stupid." That's what I teach my salesmen. I think that's the only rule prayer really requires. If you start making it complicated, people start getting concerned about whether they're doing it right.

I'm glad we were keeping it simple three years ago. That's when the bottom dropped out of the nation's business, and that's when I found myself without a job for nearly a year. That was a long, long year.

We weren't in a critical financial bind or afraid of going hungry, but I questioned my ability, my adequacy—even my manhood.

When we lay in bed at night and prayed, I said things in the presence of my wife that I'd never say in front of anyone else.

No question about it, I feel totally safe with Jackie.

I wonder sometimes how I'd know her or how she'd know me if we didn't pray together. I wonder if I'd say *to* her some of the things I said to God *with* her when I was without a job.

When you pray with someone, you get down to where they live inside themselves. And you let them into that place inside yourself.

It's something—I mean, it's really something—to have Jackie hold my hand and pray to the Father from deep inside herself.

We're enormously closer because of our prayer. No question in my mind.

JACKIE: I felt closer to Bob because I *knew* him better. Of course, anyone would know he was upset about his loss of a job. But if we hadn't prayed together, I don't think I'd have known what it was really like for him down deep.

And I wouldn't have known that he was so concerned about other jobless people. Even after Bob began his new job, we continued to pray for jobless friends. And jobless strangers, too. He would call people—one person in particular—who were out of work. He'd call maybe once a week because he knew what it was like and he knew they needed to talk.

I learned to know my husband on a new level during that period.

I think we also come to know God better than I ever would just in private prayer. I guess I could say I get a man's viewpoint, a husband's, a father's viewpoint. As strong as Bob is in the way he handles things, he's also a tender husband and father. I've become more aware of those qualities in God the Father. God is strong and also tender.

BOB: Unity is what marriage is all about in God's plan. This is a second marriage for both of us and I'm grateful to God for giving us this second chance to find that kind of unity in Christian marriage.

It's been hard sometimes, being a father and a stepfather. Sometimes I feel awful that I can't do for my own kids what I can do for the boys (Jackie's sons). There've been other things, too. I'm stricter than Jackie. Sometimes the boys will go to Jackie and I get a kind of left-out feeling.

That's the kind of thing that can make second marriages really sticky and cause a kind of distance between a couple. Thank God Jackie and I can pray honestly about it. I don't mean to say we never disagree or misunderstand. We do. But we don't keep it inside and it doesn't separate us. Actually, when we pray about these things, we become closer.

JACKIE: I really believe God wants couples to pray. It's sort of what unity means. You have to spend quality time together to be friends. You have to share, be open, listen. Praying with Bob has deepened our friendship and helped me be almost constantly aware of God's friendship with us.

"We've Been Stealing Missalettes"

"Not long ago, I read this piece in America *magazine called 'Steal a Missalette,' so that's what we've been doing. We've stolen two so far. Each one has the daily Mass readings for several months. We begin our prayer time by reading the Scripture assigned for that day."* David Russell

David and Joyce Russell, in their early thirties, have three children aged six, four, and six months. The Russells met at Marquette University where they were working toward master's degrees in English. When they married eight years ago, they began life together with fuzzy plans to combine two careers, marriage, parenting, and church involvement into some kind of nearly effortless harmony. That plan didn't work out! Joyce's work as a radio anchor newscaster in the evenings and David's decision to divide his days among college teaching, parenting, cooking, and writing resulted in a fractured schedule with little quality time together. That situation, combined with a recent move and the birth of their third child, has resulted in a lengthy period of painful reorganization. That is where we meet them in this interview.

DAVID: We're just beginners. We're just waking up. We've said, over and over, both of us, that it's as though we've been asleep and are just now waking up. We've been sleep-walking during the first eight years of our marriage. We made a lot of mistakes while we were sleep-walking.

23

JOYCE: Yes, we are beginners. That's startling to me. I thought that since we went to church together and prayed before meals, we were a prayerful couple. We've been active in the church and we've been in prayer groups. Each of us has prayed privately. We both have well-worn Bibles. So it's been quite shocking to me to realize that we haven't really prayed together.

We did pray some during our engagement and early marriage. When I look back on those times, it was almost like a performance: me performing for David and David performing for me. Now I'm praying to God with David, and that's a far better prayer than I ever prayed before.

I still have to fight off shyness in order to pray in front of David. It's very difficult for me to open up like that. When I do break through that wall of shyness in our prayer, it's easier to stay open to him during the day.

This has been the most difficult period of our marriage. We're dealing with a lot of mistakes we've made with career decisions and raising our children and relating to each other. All these things have come together at the same time. With a new baby in the house! For the first time, we're seriously asking: Where have we been? Where are we going? Where do we want to be when we're forty? Fifty? The pressures are so great and the questions seem so unanswerable. It's the kind of situation that could lead to divorce.

DAVID: Out of the blue one day, Joyce said, "This is where couples get divorced, isn't it?"

I remember once—I think it was Holy Week and I must've forgotten to steal a missalette—we didn't have the readings so we read the penitential psalms. It was as though those psalms voiced what was in our hearts. That's kind of where we were at the time: in the pit crying for help out of the depths, wrestling with our past mistakes and who we are and where we're going.

One of the hard things is that it's likely I'll have to make a move away from my career.

Last week a lot of the readings had to do with the vine bearing fruit. As we talked, we decided we are at a point where God is pruning us back and getting unnecessary things out of the way so we can bear fruit in our marriage the way God wants us to.

I wonder if we'd be praying as a couple now if Bryan and Sandy Mize (friends in St. Louis) hadn't encouraged us. Early in our marriage, we were in a prayer group with Bryan and Sandy and two other couples and some singles. We'd get together once a week and read the Bible and pray and have pot luck. We prayed a lot in that group but we didn't usually pray at home.

When we began going through this tough period, we mentioned our struggle to Bryan and Sandy. In our correspondence since then, Bryan told us that he and Sandy have been praying together and reading the Scripture each morning. Then, in a way that's quite unlike him—he's not one to give unsolicited advice!—he really encouraged us to pray. He sounded like a salesman.

The form of our prayer is based on what they do. They use the daily Mass readings, so we've been "stealing" missalettes so we can find the daily readings.

We wake up and say this little prayer—I don't remember where we got it—"As morning breaks, we look to you, O Lord, to be our strength this day." We say this as our eyes open—if they do open. Whoever is most awake starts it, and we say it together.

We sit on the couch in the family room upstairs and close the door. Sometimes John (6) or Mary (4) will interrupt us for something, but they have quickly come to realize that this is our special time.

We read the readings for that day. Sometimes we'll talk about what strikes us in a reading. Sometimes we just pause.

Then we just pray. Out loud. There are days we thank God a lot. Other days, it's a kind of gimmie prayer—a we're-in-trouble-again prayer. We always try to remember people we know who are sick or hurting or trying to make decisions the way we're trying to do. We haven't reached the point where we pray much about cosmic things or global things.

JOYCE: We believe it's important to pray every day. That was hard for us because of our schedules. Part of our "reform" was rearranging our schedule. We resolved to get up at the same time and to have time together. We are now definitely committed to praying together regularly.

Although this has been the most difficult period of our marriage, it has also been a blessed time. I really feel—this may sound shocking—but I really feel that I'm completely committed to our marriage for the first time.

I can also say that there's much more joy in our lives than there was five or six months ago. Probably a deeper joy than any we experienced in our first eight years. We're still dealing with serious things, but we're dealing in a different way.

We are becoming more like-minded. More and more we echo one another's prayer. David's prayer is my prayer, and I find myself saying "Yes, Lord," while David prays.

We've been more supportive of one another in the past few months than ever before in our marriage. It goes along with my sense that—for the first time, really—I am committed to our marriage—and with my awareness that I was holding back during the first eight years.

We also pray together other times, these days. Most nights, we pray. In bed. Just a short, simple prayer. And during the day, when we sit down to talk over something important, one of us will say, "Let's pray before we talk about this."

DAVID: Yes, we talk more than we ever have before about what's deeply important to us. There's a huge difference. Sometimes we have very strong discussions: debating an issue, arguing, complaining. I think these conversations are, in a sense, a continuation of the prayer that began in the morning.

I'm learning to be more responsible in our marriage than I ever was. Praying to God with Joyce causes me to really consider what I say. I'm less able to be proud or perfunctory with God. Less able to fool myself.

Before we began talking and praying the way we do now, God, to me, had more to do with religion or theology. Now I understand that God has more to do with the way we live all day.

JOYCE: There's one thing I feel a need for. I need support from other couples who pray together. I'd like to hear them talk about how they pray, about the benefits and difficulties. It would help me to know we're not doing something odd. That might sound funny. I've prayed all my life—at least off and on. So why would praying with my husband be odd. Yet I need—or at least I'd like—to talk with other couples who pray together.

I think part of this feeling comes from my awareness that we've made some decisions poorly without feedback from family and friends. Now we are consciously trying to change that and not do things in isolation.

One help to us has been the friends we've made in the parish. It's easier for us not to be isolated as a couple when we have friends in common. We each have maintained old friendships that pre-date our marriage, but for a while we did not have common couple friends who share our values. Our life is touched by friends we've made—especially among the Young Marrieds [a parish group]. I think those kinds of friendships can help us maintain our life of prayer.

DAVID: The day we moved into this house, the reading was about Jesus telling Zacchaeus to come down out of the sycamore tree and Jesus saying, "I want to go to your house." There's a big sycamore tree in our yard, and I prayed that day that Jesus would do that, that he'd come into our house. I'm beginning to see what that means. Jesus isn't just in the church; he's here—in all homes where he's invited. He wants to come in.

"Once You Turn God Loose, It Boggles Your Mind"

> *"When I was a kid, I could put walls around God and not let him get any bigger than that. But once you turn God loose, it boggles your mind. As I learn about other people's God—the way they know him—he gets bigger and bigger. He's out of the box. I can't comprehend what God is like anymore. I just believe."* Don Baustert

Don Baustert—bearded, meditative, and German—grew up in the country where he worked in flat cotton fields. Linda McKenna—feisty, warm, fair-skinned and Irish—grew up in a sprawling city and could find her way by bus to almost any point on the tangled urban streets.

Twenty-three years ago, Don and Linda met and married. They have four children. Linda is a nurse and works in geriatrics. Don manages a data system at a local air force base.

Recently, the Bausterts have experienced some changes in their family life: their youngest daughter, Laura, contracted chronic hepatitis and is still in treatment; the three older children are finishing college and moving away from home; Don's mom died and his dad came to live with them.

Linda and Don deal with these changes in ways typical of them. Linda tunes in to the adjustments and needs of each family member and worries with great gusto over each one. Don rolls with the punches and reflects on the larger meanings of life events. They have developed these complementary patterns over the years.

29

LINDA: We made a Retorno ten years ago, but it didn't take. I was uncomfortable with it.

Before that, the only time we'd ever prayed out loud together was when Don's sister, Janie, was sick. It was hard for me. Embarrassing, like the first time we stood naked before each other. I thought, "I bet this sounds real stupid to Don." It was the hardest thing I've done, to open my mouth and say those words. It's funny, because I'd learned to pray in a group when we worked Marriage Encounter weekends. But just Don and me, alone in a room, to reach way down inside and pull it up and say, "This is what I believe"—that was hard.

Later we made another Retorno, and that one took. We made a commitment then to pray together regularly. And we have. That was nine years ago.

But for a while, I was still uncomfortable because the method we learned in Retorno emphasized listening to God speak to you through Scripture. Well, God never said anything to me, but he talked to Don all the time. After we'd read the Scripture, I'd say, "You go first," because I hadn't heard a thing. Then Don would say all this beautiful stuff and I'd think, "How come you say so much to Don and don't say anything to me?" I'd usually end up in a huff.

But we kept at it and finally it dawned on me that God spoke to me through Don, so I relaxed. Even now, I usually get my first insights from Don. After that, I can often take it farther and deeper.

At first, we had a struggle to find a time and place to pray. Individual private prayer you can do just about any time or place—even walking down the street. But for couple prayer, we had to prioritize our time. Evenings didn't work out. It was hard to find the energy after the world had wracked us around for a day.

For us, it boiled down to my having to get up early. Don is disciplined. He's disciplined in his eating. He's disciplined in his exercise. So to get up earlier was easy for him. I'm not disciplined at all. I didn't think I could do it. But once I made up my mind, it really wasn't that hard. And I'm a lot nicer, too, since I started getting up early. I have more energy.

Our prayer isn't very formal at all. It's just kind of a three-way conversation. We usually use the Scripture. Twice we went through that little book, *God Speaks.* Then we read a lot of the Bible, a book at a time, reading a little each morning. We started with Jeremiah and Isaiah and then we went to the New Testament. Now we pick one of the Scripture readings for the day.

DON: To me, I think couple prayer has two parts. That time when Linda and I and God sit down together in the morning is just one part. The other part happens all day long.

It's like chopping cotton. You work those long rows in the hot sun, and then you have to find a shade tree and sit down. Chopping cotton *takes* energy. Resting in the shade *restores* energy. Our morning prayer is shade-tree time. It helps us on the road. It gives us energy to keep chopping that cotton. That's the other part of prayer.

When I leave the house in the morning, it seems as though everybody needs a piece of me. When I come back home in the evening, I'm tired. Sometimes I feel like that guy in Scripture who lay down under the broom tree and would just as soon die as live. He took a nap and ate some bread and drank some water and got it back together again. That's what we do in couple prayer. It helps us walk forty days and forty nights the way Whoever-It-Was did in Scripture. I get that energy from God and from Linda.

Words without action—that's not prayer to my way of thinking. Your whole day is—or can be—a prayer. I can pray for someone who is sick or lonely, but if I don't get off my butt and go visit them, those words are meaningless.

Prayer is how well you treat your kids. To spend time with them. To come home dead tired and still go out and play baseball with them.

Prayer means to listen to someone tell a story for the eight hundredth time because he still needs to talk. There's a guy at work whose wife died. I walk with him at noon every day; and for thirty minutes a day for two years he talked out his pain. I think that was a prayer.

Prayer means to accept. When I was growing up, we had an old Belgian priest who was probably the cause of all the struggles I had with religion and God. He preached a very harsh God, and it took me fifteen years to get over what he taught me. Someone called a couple of years ago and said he was dying, so I went to the hospital to see him. That old turkey didn't believe anything he'd taught me! He told me about how happy he was with his new belief in God. He and I had taken some different roads to get out of that theological jungle and get to the same God. I visited him a lot. Our sharing was a prayer.

Even the party in our new house last night was a big prayer. People came in and listened. They hugged and talked. They cared. They got energy from one another. Of course we don't have much energy left today—but that party was a big prayer meeting.

Yeah, for me, if Linda and I aren't involved with God's people, we aren't praying. When we pray as a couple, we support each other and give each other energy. I go out into my day and get involved; she goes out into her day. When we pray, we take all that and weave it together.

LINDA: I think Don's right about that. I don't know if we reach out to others any more than we used to; but since we have been praying together, I'm much more aware that this apology or that visit is God's work in the world.

Don and I still have really different concepts of God. My idea of God is that he's like a loving parent of small children.

I petition him a lot. Don hardly ever petitions. Don listens and praises.

In my family, you didn't leave the house to go two doors down the street without my daddy putting the sign of the cross on your forehead. It was almost magical. I was safe if my daddy blessed me. It's the same way with God. I believe in miracles. In my heart, I believe for example that God could step in and heal Laura's liver, and I keep asking him to do that.

When Laura got sick, I got very angry with this God who, to me, is like a miracle-working, loving parent. I couldn't pray to him. I had nothing to say to him. I couldn't understand how this loving God I'd finally gotten to know—how he could let this happen to a little girl who had never done anything to him!

Don and I would sit down together in the mornings to read Scripture and I couldn't even see the words. Don would read. Don would share. Don would pray. And I'd sit there and cry. I bet you, for six months straight I sat and cried every morning while Don prayed for the two of us.

But I think if we hadn't had that time together—well, I wonder if I could've made it. Don was so gentle. He never once said, "Now, Linda, this is stupid. Get your act together." He just supported me and loved me. So our prayer time really held me together.

Don's concept of God is different. Don says, "God will take care of us in his own way. He just wants us to chop our cotton every day, and he'll do what he's going to do." Don's really practical. He believes in leaving alone the things you can't do anything about. He says, "Why wear yourself out trying to do what only God can do?" But I keep trying. I worry. I come from a worrying family.

This difference in the way we see God wasn't so clear to us before we started praying together. We talked *about* God a lot in those first fourteen years, but we didn't hear one another talk *to* God the way we do now.

I think we've both expanded our ideas of God. There have been lots of other changes, but they happen so gradually, I never stop to analyze them unless we sit down and talk about it the way we're doing now.

One change that's really clear to me is our closeness. We've always been close—good friends—but we used to get mad at each other more and stay mad longer. I think God uses couple prayer as a vehicle to help us resolve differences in our relationship.

Praying together takes away the need to put up defenses. You don't tattle on each other when you pray. You look into yourself.

It's hard—if not impossible—to sit down together and listen to Don's God and listen to my God and form a prayer together—and get up still angry with one another.

Part of the healing, I think, comes from touch. Don and I sit next to each other on the couch, so we're touching. When we pray, we *always* touch. That's our signal. We'll either hold hands or something. You can't stay mad when you're touching like that.

Sex is better, too. I'm sure there's a connection but I can't put it into words.

DON: Sure, sex is better. When you share your core—including the dark stuff, you know, your fears and doubts and hurts—and someone accepts all that, then the physical act of intercourse has got to be better. There's not so much garbage hidden away. It's a freer act. There's more to celebrate. I mean, someone knows you all the way to the bottom and accepts you all the way to the bottom. I mean, *that* is unity.

It's easier to be friends, too. If you know people's toads, they're easier to love. Toads are part of our humanity. We're not perfect and we don't love perfect people. But sometimes we pretend a lot. When Linda and I pray, we reveal our toads. That's what we love in each other.

Another thing, I think our prayer has affected our kids. They all love to worship. Even before Linda and I began couple prayer, going to church on Sunday as a family was a celebration. They've never once complained about going to church.

Both boys are prayerful but in real different ways. Dale loves to hear the monks chant at St. Gregory's. Both of them often go to Mass during the week. So does Lisa.

But to get back to what I think is the most important thing for our couple relationship: to me, in couple prayer, you share that part of yourself you probably haven't shared—ever—with any other human being, maybe that part of yourself that's a little bit dark and that you don't even understand. Usually, that's the part that makes you different from anyone else. You probably share it, if at all, with only one other person in your whole lifetime.

I always knew Linda was a caring person, but now I see the depth of it. God, how she loves those old people she works with. The sick neighbor. Our kids. Me. That's her godliness. That's a piece of God in her. I can sort of understand, then, for a while, what God is 'like. He loves like that and more. Then it gets away from me. I can't get my arms around the idea of that much love.

"It's Hard To Pray
Together When You're Angry"

"This morning I felt irritated with Lisa and I went through this, 'Shall I try to clear the air now and then pray? If I do, will we be able to pray after I unload?' I took the risk and then we were able to pray together. This morning, at least, it worked out. It doesn't always. It's hard to pray when you're angry." Mike Smith

Mike Smith is thirty years old. His wife, Lisa White Smith, is twenty-eight. They have two very small children with very long names: Hannah Elisa White Smith, age three, and Luke Michael White Smith, age one.

Mike and Lisa, both musicians, both idealists, have pieced together three church-related jobs which they share. This arrangement enables one of them to be home with their children most of the time. It also enables them to fulfill their desire to be engaged in church ministry.

Most of their work is related to liturgy to which they bring not only good music but also a deep understanding of worship.

Mike recently finished a master's degree in social work. Lisa is considering working toward a counseling degree. These new directions in learning simply mean new possibilities in ministry.

LISA: During my childhood, we'd say grace before meals and go to church on Sundays. I was satisfied with that. Then, when I was in high school, my mom and dad had a significant religious experience related to the charismatic renewal. It was as though overnight, their lives—and ours, too—changed.

We were living in Europe at the time. My father was up for bird colonel—he would've been one of the youngest colonels in the air force—and was making lots of money.

Overnight, all that changed. The week before his promotion, he announced that he was retiring. He was going to become a religious educator!

It was beyond me. I was horrified. I can't tell you what a crisis it was for me. I was so wrapped up in status.

I thought they were kooks. *Kooks!* Even their language changed. At dinner the night after their big change, instead of "NameFatherSonHolySpiritBlessusOLord" it was "Let's hold hands and take turns thanking God." I thought, "What are we doing? We've done it this way every day of our lives." Everything was upside down. They would ask me, "What's the Lord doing in your life?" They had never asked that! They were so excited. I was so cynical.

Sure enough, Dad got out and we moved back to the states. Both of them worked together as religious educators.

Looking back, I can see this had an influence on me. I got through my adolescence and made peace with the changes. And later I had a religious awakening, too.

Mom and Dad became a model for me. Mom still does parish work. They still pray together. They're very faithful about it—but, then, they don't have Hannah and Luke to interrupt them!

Mike and I met at a retreat. From the very beginning, we had a spiritual bond. We had an on-again off-again relationship.

We argued a lot. About God! God was a hot topic for us. Mike was more in tune with God as a God of justice and equality, and he would raise questions of sexism in the church. I remember one day in the living room before we were married, Mike said something about the Father, the Son, and "the mothering Spirit"! I said, "What? The *mothering* Spirit!" We really argued then.

We were at OSU. We were both in charismatic prayer groups, so prayer and faith sharing were easy for us. We didn't always like one another well enough to pray together, but the actual act of praying together was never awkward for us.

We don't belong to a charismatic prayer group now, but our prayer life is certainly different because of that. The greatest gift it gave us was freedom of prayer. We used to see peace and justice work as focused on issues and the charismatic renewal as focused on prayer. But now peace work seems to have become much more prayerful and we like *that* combination. We still work at the Peace House but not as much as we did before we had kids. The charismatic renewal, well, it comes down to an awakening of the Spirit in our lives. That was our gift. That was the gift to the Church.

MIKE: Lisa and I married five years ago. I didn't marry her just in order to be married. I married because Lisa was there. It was a sense of call. Our shared spiritual values were a big attraction, but we were also in love. I thought about her and longed for her. Religion and love brought us together. A good example is our wedding night. We prayed that night. We also drank a bottle of champagne.

Our first year was very difficult.

We both felt called to ministry in the church, so when we got a job offer in a parish, we took it.

Looking back, I don't know how we prayed together that year, but we did. It was just a discipline. We were really stressed. New jobs. New home. No friends. Working in the institutional church. Being together twenty-four hours a day. Going home together with stress and anger from work. And just not knowing what being married really means.

I can remember, we'd sit down to pray. We knew it was important. But it was hard. We just made ourselves do it.

Finally, almost exactly one year later, it was over. It was as though one day peace was upon our house. We were relating and understanding.

We were still disillusioned in our work, however.

Most of the people who have encouraged us to work in the church have been women religious. "You are a sign of hope for the church," they'd say. "Get on out there!" So we do. We're excited. We feel called to ministry. Then we get into it, and what a disappointment. And we say, "Why did they encourage us like that? They knew what it's like! It was a dirty trick!"

We aren't through the disillusion yet. Some days we're able to say, "Well, the church is a community of saints and sinners, and that's just life." Other days, we say, "This is ridiculous and I don't know why we're sticking to it. And God, please tell us what to do."

LISA: Mike is right. The disillusion has been very hard for us. One thing that makes it difficult is that a lot of our work is related to liturgy—and liturgy is clergy turf! When I worked with the elderly or when we did campus ministry, it was okay. But it's not always okay for us to plan a liturgy. Of course this isn't always true. We find a lot of support and encouragement from some clergy. As Mike said, we pray about it a lot.

After we were married, we began praying the Liturgy of the Hours and we still do. It gives us a structure for our prayer, but it also gives us the flexibility to incorporate shared prayer. We read the Scripture for the day—the Mass readings—and we discuss it. That's what we've done since marriage.

We used to do just Evening Prayer. But since the kids came, it's been very difficult. It's ended up more now that we pray Morning Prayer because the kids—well, we can usually beat them up.

First thing in the morning, we get a cup of coffee. Then we pray.

We pray differently now than we did before we married and during most of the first year of marriage. That was not really intimate prayer. I guess you could say it was couple prayer because a couple was doing it, but it was not intimate couple prayer. Now our prayer together puts us in touch with one another. We know each other's concerns and needs and feelings.

Mike said something this morning that really struck me. He said, "Prayer puts us in touch with who we are and what we are about; and, as a couple, it puts us in touch with who we are *as a couple* and what we are about as a couple."

I feel a union with Mike. After morning prayer, I have a sense of being with Mike. It pervades the whole day.

I think Mike has the same experience. I might say, in prayer, "I'm feeling bad about myself today." We may not have talked about that, so we reveal current feelings that way.

But we don't reveal anything big during prayer. I think that's because we just keep current. So there are no surprises.

Another thing, when I have a pain or concern, I can share it with God and Mike, and vice versa. But when we both have the same pain, we're taking it someplace. We're not just batting it back and forth. We have that sense of peace when we present it to God together.

MIKE: Our personal relationship with God is important, and we each have our own responsibility to take care of that. So coming together to pray is, in one sense, just sharing with Lisa what I have shared with God.

Hannah "prays" with us sometimes. She saw us with our prayer books. We'd say "Can you be quiet now for a little bit? We're going to pray." She didn't like that. I guess she felt excluded. She had one of those little pocket Bibles the Gideons put out. So she got that, and she'd keep it with our book.

When we'd sit down to pray, she'd get that little bitty Bible and sit there with us for five or ten minutes. She still does it once in a while.

Praying together helps us make decisions about life-style kinds of things. Often an insight will come in the faith-sharing part of our prayer.

For instance, we feel called to simple living. In our couple prayer, we challenge one another to be faithful to that—even in small ways, such as using what we have wisely or planting a garden. This ideal began with a desire to sort out what is the kingdom the Gospel talks about and how do you live it in North America in 1986—and realizing we're living in the kingdom now and it's not something I get to when I die.

We don't do a good job of living up to our ideal. We have the desire, but we don't always do it.

But once the kids came and we changed jobs and took a drastic cut in pay, we were happier. It seemed easier to value other things. We feel lucky to be able to share our jobs and stay home with our kids more. Many couples have the same desire, but just aren't able to do it. We're lucky to have the kind of set-up we have.

LISA: We have a need for community. A big part of our prayer is our plea for some experience of community, some sense of support that a parish can't seem to offer. We seldom feel any kind of oneness with other lay persons—married couples who experience life in a way similar to the way we do. What makes it worse is that we believe we're *supposed* to be in community. We *long* for community. But we can't find it.

"You Can't Pray Lies"

*"Praying together keeps us honest. If I don't pray about
what's deep inside me, it's because I haven't become conscious of it yet. When I am conscious of what's going on
inside me, whether I like it or not, I pray about it. You
can't pretend to be different. You can't pray lies."* Rita
Galier

Vic and Rita Galier have been married twenty-six years.
They have six children and a grandson.

Standing erect, Rita (forty-five) measures exactly five
feet. Gravel-voiced Vic (forty-seven) towers over her at six feet
four and a half inches, and he weighs in at two hundred and
ninety pounds.

Rita says they are just about as different in their backgrounds as in their sizes. Although both are cradle-Catholics,
Vic grew up in a free-and-easy family that saw life in "lots of
gray," whereas Rita grew up in a family that lived "by the law"
and saw life in black and white. Through the close exchange of
twenty-six years of marriage, they view life now in a more similar way.

Vic is a permanent deacon. Rita participated in all the diaconate studies and she and Vic share most of the ministry assigned to Vic.

Two years ago, Vic learned that he had lung cancer. He
was told he had nine months to live. The crisis brought them
both to a keener appreciation of the value of couple prayer.

VIC: We've been praying as a couple all our married life. We started on our wedding night. I think we picked it up from Rita's folks. They used to pray every night.

Basically, all we did for a while was rote prayer and maybe a simple thank you. We prayed like that for years. Then we began going to a charismatic prayer group and that changed our couple prayer a little. The big turn around was when we got involved in Retorno—that was eight years ago. That's when we began praying with Scripture.

I think couple prayer has held us closer—even held us to-gether. I mean way back. The first seven years—well, there were some hard times.

Early back, after we began a more conversational style of prayer, I'd sometimes not pray about something because I wouldn't want to say it to Rita. Then I got to thinking, "I'm holding back from God, too. And from myself." I was playing games—sort of like "If I don't talk about it, it won't be." As we got deeper into our prayer, it was easier to just go ahead and say it, whether God liked it or not. Being able to talk about everything has made us tremendously more aware of what's going on with each other.

RITA: My parents still pray. In my family, when I was grow-ing up, we didn't close doors much. I could hear my parents praying at night. It was a very comforting sound. Sometimes they'd invite us, and we'd all go in and sit on their bed. They read from the Bible and from a book called *The Upper Room.*

Vic and I pray the same way—except that we later settled on early morning as our time. At night, it got to be too long. I'd fall asleep. We said, "Phooey on that!"

We pray in our bedroom. That's where we've always prayed. Now when mother and dad visit us, we invite *them* into *our* bedroom and we all sit around in our nightgowns and pray.

We even used, for a long time, *The Upper Room*. It comes out every two months, and it has a Scripture reading and a reflection. We talk about what we heard in the Scripture and then we pray.

I think you can handle all of life if you're honest. It's dishonesty you can't deal with.

Sometimes things—even things about ourselves—are hidden. Reflecting out loud helps me find out what's really going on. Sometimes I'll tell Vic, "I don't know what's wrong. I just feel as though a cloud is around me and I don't know why." When we talk about it, we can usually trace the feeling. If I don't find it out and deal with it, it can develop into a separation between us.

VIC: I think our prayer life was really good until we got into the diaconate program. It began to suffer then because we were so busy studying and reading. Our first course was in the Hebrew Scriptures.

We began listening to Scripture with a different ear, you might say. We began to analyze. To a degree, it ruined our prayer life!

RITA: That's right. That first summer of diaconate study, we continued the couple prayer we'd grown used to. Then we were given the Common Prayer Book, so we added Morning Prayer, Afternoon Prayer, and Evening Prayer—and Mass in between! By the end of the first week, we were saying "Lord, deliver us from all this prayer."

We told Joe [Father Joe Ross] that we were just prayed out.

Besides that, we'd grown used to conversational prayer, and to use the Common Prayer Book was like going back to rote prayer.

But the study of Scripture *had* to enhance our prayer. Subconsciously we have it in the back of our heads and it helps us understand the real meaning. We're not inclined to be as fundamental as we used to be. It was just that it took us a while to put our old prayer system and our new knowledge together.

There are times we don't pray. That's usually when one of us is mad, and we'll feel separated in a way. It might last a week; it might be three days. I don't think we withhold prayer as a conscious way to get even—such as someone getting mad and saying "Okay, I'm just not going to have sex with you." For us, our intimate space is prayer, and *that's* what we quit doing together when we're separated by anger. It's not a way to get even; it just doesn't fit.

We often end those times of separation through prayer. If Vic has been mad at me, for example, he might get up one morning and say, "Let's pray this morning." That's the start. It never fails—it *never* fails—that reconciliation takes place.

As far as sex, I'd say our prayer life and our sex life always go hand in hand. When we're angry, we don't pray and we don't make love. When we're united, both are good.

That's another reason I like having just the two of us pray. We pray with our door open, and the kids can come in, and that's okay. But it's different. They seem to appreciate that our couple prayer is special.

VIC: Talking about our children, one week our parish had a week of renewal with different speakers every night. One— Father Pribil—said that parents are given a special power by God to bless their children. I thought that was very neat. After that, when I was around one of the kids, I'd just sometimes put my hands on their head or put my arms around them and say a silent prayer.

After we made our second Retorno, I shared that with our kids—told them what I'd been doing.

One morning, during our quiet time, our oldest daughter, who was a high school senior then, knocked on our door and said, "Mom, Daddy, as soon as you finish your quiet time, can I come in and get your blessing. I'm going to have a real hard day."

That meant a lot to us.

Our kids' closeness has been a real blessing since I got sick.

Two years ago, the doctors gave me nine months to live. They said, "Your cancer is inoperable. It does not respond well to treatment. Prepare your affairs."

That weekend after I came home from the hospital, I baptized my grandbaby. I told everyone at the ceremony that he was my sign of trust. He was so helpless and he had to trust his father and mother. I was helpless, too; I had to trust my Father.

My daughter kept him around me quite a bit. He's a very special little guy to me.

At first, when people would ask me about my condition, I'd say, "I trust in my God and whatever God wills will be done." Then I began to count the months, two months, three months that had gone by, and it was harder to say that.

Sometimes I would keep myself awake all night because I was afraid I wouldn't wake up if I let go. There was no foundation to that idea. It was pure fear.

Four months after the diagnosis, I went to a charismatic group that Tom Schott [a friend and fellow deacon] belongs to and asked them to pray over me. We went back a few weeks later to praise God. The cancer was in remission. It's been two years since the doctor told me I had nine months to live.

RITA: I shudder to think what would have happened if we hadn't had a life of prayer when Vic got sick. We knew that God was active in our lives and that God's plan was being worked out.

We had learned to pray aloud together about whatever was deep inside us. We cried pillows full—both of us—during that time. We'd start praying and start crying. We told God our fear, our anger, everything.

The day Vic came home from the hospital Ken [Father Kulinski, a close friend] and the doctor came over and just sat with the family. We hadn't yet had a chance as a family to debrief. We all talked about how angry and scared and sad we were. Our youngest son got up and left. He said, "I don't want to hear any more." But he came back in pretty soon. We shared all these feelings early on, so they didn't fester in us.

Vic's cancer has spread to his brain and into his bones. But lately his pain seems less heavy and his energy level is up. You'd think we'd be thinking of the big things, like life and death. We do. But we also still struggle to work out the dailiness of things. It's as though we've shifted roles, and that's been awkward, especially when I've begun to take care of things that Vic has always done and then he gets to feeling better and wants me to do those things his way. We still pray about those kinds of issues, as well as praying about our ministry.

VIC: Rita and I have talked a lot about why God has given me this extension. We think it's because the Lord has given us a special ministry. I can't do anything long range, so we visit the sick and shut-in parishioners. They are sort of the invisible people; and when I'm strong enough, we visit them. But a really special ministry has become clear to us: helping families plan the funeral when someone dies—to help them plan it in a way that really, really celebrates the fact of the resurrection. We've had three or four unexpected deaths in our parish this year, and we've felt good about praying with those families and helping them plan the funeral. I never thought about that as a special ministry before, but now I do. Maybe it's because I'm so aware of my own mortality. And immortality!

Yeah, prayer has been a very special gift in our lives. More couples need that. But couples have to come up with their own spirituality. Couples can't pray the way the monk prays in the monastery or the way Sister Mary prays. We have to pray the way *we* pray.

Part Two

Reflections for Couples Who Pray Together: Dialogical Prayer

Like making love or sharing secrets, praying together is an act of intimacy. It could be said of each of these acts that couples do it because they are intimate, and they become intimate because they do it.

Good-marriage intimacy is a special kind of friendship.

In the past decade, among the welter of books on problem marriages, there have been some shining studies of happy marriages. By "happy" marriages we mean those in which both persons feel comfortable, committed, and content. The mark of a good marriage is not ecstacy, but unity. Almost every happily married couple interviewed in these studies ranked friendship as the number one reason they were happy together.

In friendship, couples freely exchange thoughts, feelings, values, dreams, and desires. They talk. They listen. Small wonder that marriage enrichment programs emphasize communication and that a goodly portion of successful marriage counseling is geared to reducing the blocks that hinder communication.

Although there are probably dozens of approaches to marriage communication, two "rules" emerge as basic: 1. talk-to-tell, and 2. listen-to-learn. These same two rules apply to prayer.

This neat system of talking and listening is called dialogue. Dialogue takes energy. We can't always be in dialogue.

We would be worn to a frazzle in two days! So between genuine dialogues, we chit-chat, exchange information, joke, and
comment. Nevertheless, if dialogue happens frequently
enough, the entire relationship abides in a climate of dynamic
honesty; and when appropriate times come, we can leave the
level of chit-chat and get down to the business of dialogue.

Let us look first at how the two rules of dialogue apply to
marriage. Then we can more easily see how they also apply to
couple prayer.

Both talking-to-tell and listening-to-learn require an attitude of discovery.

Before we talk, we must first discover what we really do
think or feel. We take time enough and we reflect enough to
find that out. If we come to this self-knowledge and don't say
it, the knowledge stays inside us and we are not fully known.
If we say it accurately—that is, if we talk-to-tell—our partners
know us better. What's more, we know ourselves better, for
sharing clarifies.

There are risks in talking to tell.

For one thing, it makes us more clearly known, and to be
known is to be more vulnerable. We all carry the marks of our
own humanness, which is to say we all are weak as well as
strong, petty as well as noble, confused as well as certain. To
put all that into words is a risk.

Another risk is the call to grow. The risk of conversion. If
I discover, for example, that I sometimes behave out of jeal-
ousy, and if I put that discovery into words, I can no longer
behave that way without both of us being more aware and less
comfortable with what I am doing. The discovery and the talking form a challenge to grow.

Like talking-to-tell, listening-to-learn also requires a
sense of discovery. This kind of listening is much more com-
plex than converting sound waves into sense. It involves an
almost detective-like curiosity.

*What do you really mean? When and how did this value
or notion or desire become important to you? How important
is it? What goes on in your gut when you talk about this? What
pictures, or expectations, do you have in your head? I want to
know these things because I want to know you. Sure, we
shared big hunks of information before we married and for a
time after that. But that doesn't mean I now know you forever
and ever, amen. Knowing you is an ongoing discovery because
you are an ongoing person. So tell me.*

This sense of discovery can enable us momentarily to put
aside our own reactions so we can be fully present to our partners. Nothing stops discovery like stopped communication,
and one of the most effective ways to stop communication is to
begin formulating a response without really hearing. Haven't
we all done that—while someone is still talking to us, we are
busy composing a reply and so miss half the message? Being
engaged in discovery requires our being fully present.

Just as there are risks in talking-to-tell, there is risk in listening-to-learn. What we hear can call us to grow. Growth
means change, and change is nearly always uncomfortable.

For example, a wife may be called to let go of her I'm-
right-you're-wrong attitude because by really listening, she
understands that her husband is right, too, and that it's not a
matter of right and wrong but simply a matter of difference.
That's hard. It's a lot easier to feel justified by hanging onto
one's "rightness" than it is to work out differences.

Or a husband may be called to let go of his habit of laying
down the law because, by genuine listening, he understands
that his wife feels de-esteemed by his behavior and that she
has the capability and desire to be an equal partner in their
marriage.

Dialogue, like other intimate acts, carries the unique
stamp of those engaged in the act. Thus, each couple's dia-

logue style will be unique in some way. When they do it, how often they do it, where they do it, who initiates it, how hesitant or rushed it is, what it's about, what is learned, how the call to growth is heard: these things will vary from couple to couple. Nevertheless, if it is dialogue, the basic elements of dialogue will be there.

In summary, the elements of marriage dialogue consist of an attitude of loving discovery, the basic rules of talking-to-tell and listening-to-learn, and a response to the call to grow.

When the same attitude, rules, and response apply in couple prayer, we call that prayer dialogical. It, too, is a dialogue. God speaks-to-reveal and listens-to-hear us; we listen-to-learn God and talk-to-tell. And we are called to grow.

Sometimes we are inclined to spend our prayer time mainly explaining situations to God and asking for various kinds of favors. That's a monologue. It's one-directional. Usually in a prayer monologue, we neither talk-to-tell, getting deep inside ourselves, nor listen-to-learn, letting ourselves be changed by God's word. That kind of prayer certainly doesn't take as much energy as dialogue does!

Like marriage dialogue, we begin dialogical prayer with an attitude of discovery, a kind of searching love.

What does this word of yours really mean, Lord? How important is it in our relationship—yours with us? What do you want me to learn from the strange stories in Judges or the oracles of the prophets or the friendships of Jesus or the misadventures of Paul? I want to know you better. Sure, I learned a lot about you in religion class. But that doesn't mean I now know you forever and ever, amen. I can't sum you up like an equation or summarize you like an historical event. You are a living God. You keep telling me about yourself. I want to hear you. Help me.

And so we break open the word of God in Scripture, for Scripture is one important way God reveals himself.

Since God's relationship is different with each person, God will speak somewhat differently with each person.

Take, for example, God's word in John's Gospel, 20:19–23.

> On the evening of that day, the first day of the week, the doors being shut where the disciples were, for fear of the Jews, Jesus came and stood among them and said to them, "Peace be with you." When he had said this, he showed them his hands and his side. Then the disciples were glad when they saw the Lord. Jesus said to them again, "Peace be with you. As the Father has sent me, even so I send you." And when he had said this, he breathed on them, and said to them, "Receive the Holy Spirit. If you forgive the sins of any, they are forgiven; if you retain the sins of any, they are retained."

One listener, let's say a man, may be fearful and shut-off from family and even, to some degree, from God. He may hear God say:

I am a God who brings peace. The disciples had a big job before them; and my Son, their friend Jesus, was not there anymore. They were scared. They tried to shut people out. You know what that's like. You're closed off, too.

I will come to you anyway, in Jesus. I will come the way I came to the disciples—right through that shut door.

I come to bring you a gift: peace.

His wife may hear a different message in the same passage. Perhaps she is in turmoil because of some anger she holds against herself for some sin or mistake. She may hear God speak with her about that anger.

*Jesus is alive—as alive to you as he was to the disciples.
He still says "Peace be with you." Jesus speaks of forgiveness.
That's part of the good news: sins are forgiven. Let go of your
anger. Make room for peace.*

The same passage; different revelations.

The man in the example above may respond to God by
discovering a bit more about his defense of shutting people
out. He may meet the challenge to grow by being just a little
more open.

The woman's response will be different. She may hear
God call her to reduce the tension inside herself and in the
family by forgiving someone. She may make a small move toward reconciliation.

Two people; two responses.

Since God's revelations are different for the woman and
the man, and since their responses are different, their dialogue
with God is unique. The same Scripture passage would result
in a different dialogue with God for another couple, or even
for the same couple at a different time.

If this couple is praying together, the dialogue will be
doubly rich. More will be revealed to each of them about God
because they share their insights. They will also understand
one another in a clearer way.

Praying together can be a profoundly intimate act of marriage.

In the reflections that follow, we present some ordinary
family-life events and look at them through a scriptural lens.
Our emphasis is on listening-to-learn from God, about God.

Readers who are listening-to-learn may find in the scriptural passages messages different from the messages we high-
light. That's fine. Scripture is rich with many nuances and
levels of meaning. We present these dialogical reflections simply as models.

At the end of each Scripture reflection, we suggest various responses. This elasticity, we hope, will encourage readers to find the unique response that suits them.

Some suggested responses emphasize thanksgiving. Often a response to God's revelation may be entirely one of thanksgiving just as our response in marriage dialogue may be entirely one of appreciation.

Other suggested responses focus on a call to grow, for conversion is necessarily a part of genuine dialogue. When we really hear another, we do not remain unchanged.

Other suggestions focus on petitions, for Jesus tells us to ask the Father for what we need.

Some readers may find some suggestions helpful. Others may find that none of the suggested responses suit them. What is important in genuine dialogue is that we find words that fit what is inside of us.

One final word. We offer these prayer dialogues very tentatively and with this disclaimer: It is not our intention to present this model as the way couples should pray together. Couples do and will find their own way. What we present here is one model.

We do believe, however, that mature prayer is essentially dialogical. This is true for both liturgical and private prayer. As such, it does involve listening, responding, and conversion.

All over the city, alarms go off and sleepy-heads find their ways to kitchens to make pots of coffee or to pour orange juice or to slice bananas over cereal. All over the city, a few hours later, people begin working warmed with the coffee and energized by the caring. It's a good way to begin a day.

Married life is largely made up of such small acts. The accumulation of small everyday acts determines the quality of a marriage. If most of those acts are caring, generous, and peaceable, the marriage is likely to be unified.

Making coffee in the early morning can mean much more than simply making coffee.

2 Kings 4:42–44

A man came from Baal-shalishah, bringing the man of God bread of the first fruits, twenty loaves of barley, and fresh ears of grain in his sack. And Elisha said, "Give to the men, that they may eat." But his servant said, "How am I to set this before a hundred men?" So he repeated, "Give them to the men, that they may eat, for thus says the Lord, 'They shall eat and have some left.' " So he set it before them. And they ate, and had some left, according to the word of the Lord.

The Dialogue

We listen to God speak.

This is a little legend. I've tucked many stories in the Bible because stories are such a neat way to make a point. (If you can't say Baal-shalishah, just say Portland.)

The servant in the story is embarrassed. He thinks it would be better to offer nothing than to offer too little. But what I'm interested in is the act of offering, the generosity. So Elisha, one of my more colorful sons, insists on the offering.

I have the same message for you. Be generous. Even if you don't have much to give, I'll see that it goes very far indeed.

We respond to God.
- We let ourselves become aware of the multitude of simple things our spouses do that help us feel comfortable and cared for. We may want to thank God for our spouses.
- We are afraid to unbalance our marriage system by giving too much. Or we feel resentful toward our spouses. Or we are uncomfortable with too much closeness. So we hold back in small ways. In God's word, we hear a call to change by growing in generosity. We may ask God to help us do ordinary things with extraordinary graciousness.
- We apply the Scripture reading to our bigger family: the world. Many of our larger-family members are hungry, and we have a little to share. We thank God we can give a little and that he will make it a lot.

One thing is certain in families: people will sometimes become angry with one another. Spouses will hurt one another's feelings, kids will disappoint parents, parents will be unfair to kids.

Anger isn't all bad. Besides alerting us to disharmony in the family, it can also help us protect ourselves. Anger is a very human emotion and a helpful one, too, if we deal with it in a straightforward way.

Sometimes, however, we become angry and move into a cycle of damaging behaviors. He hurt my feelings, so I won't talk to him. She won't talk to me, so I won't make love to her. He won't make love with me, so I'll criticize him. This can go on. And on. The couple or the family gets enmeshed in this relentless pattern. The family "climate" becomes depressive.

Forgiveness changes the climate.

Forgiving is often difficult, but we can do it. God, the Forgiver, shows us how.

Ephesians 4:30–5:2

And do not grieve the Holy Spirit of God, in whom you were sealed for the day of redemption. Let all bitterness and wrath and anger and clamor and slander be put away from you, with all malice, and be kind to one another, tenderhearted, forgiving one another, as God in Christ forgave you.

Therefore be imitators of God, as beloved children. And walk in love, as Christ loved us and gave himself up for us, a fragrant offering and sacrifice to God.

The Dialogue

We listen to God speak.

I'm not asking you to get rid of anger and the behaviors that come with it just because it would be a nice thing to do. I'm telling you to get rid of it because of who you *are*. You are a person sealed with the Holy Spirit.

In biblical terms, a seal is a very personal mark showing personal possession. When you were baptized you were "sealed" by my Holy Spirit. That's not just oratory! You belong to me.

Because you bear my seal, you are to let go of these behaviors that rip people apart.

The good news is that I forgive you. The challenge is for you to forgive one another.

We respond to God.

- We have been hurt and are very angry. We don't want to lose face by giving in, but at the same time we feel miserable with the separation. We may want to pray for help in being straightforward about our hurt and anger. That's a kindness. We may also pray for help in forgiving.

- We tend to whip ourselves mentally for our past mistakes, especially those related to anger and getting even. Feeling guilty has become almost a way of life for us. In this passage, we hear God clearly say that he forgives us. We may want to praise and thank him for that.

- We understand that the power of God's seal in us goes beyond our immediate family to relatives and community. We find the hard circles of unforgiveness inside ourselves toward some of these people. We may ask the Spirit who lives and loves in us to soften these hard places.

Up to a point, worry is good. It can keep us alert and creative.

Too much worry, however, becomes anxiety and saps away our energy. Our minds become tired because we go over and over and over a problem, either remembering what did happen or fantasizing what might happen. Our bodies become tired from restless sleep and unhealthful eating and tight muscles. Exhaustion robs us of the very energy we need for coping and solving.

How do we break out of the problem-worry-exhaustion pattern? Denial will not make the problem go away. Neither will praying. God is not a genie in a magic lamp promising us a problem-free life.

What we can do is put new thoughts into our minds. For a starter, take this thought: God is with us, no matter what road we travel.

Philippians 4:4–8

Rejoice in the Lord always; again I will say, Rejoice. Let all men know your forbearance. The Lord is at hand. Have no anxiety about anything, but in everything by prayer and supplication with thanksgiving let your requests be made known to God. And the peace of God, which passes all understanding, will keep your hearts and your minds in Christ Jesus.

Finally, brethren, whatever is true, whatever is honorable, whatever is just, whatever is pure, whatever is lovely, whatever is gracious, if there is any excellence, if there is anything worthy of praise, think about these things.

The Dialogue

We listen to God speak.

If something worries you, tell me about it. Tell me with thanks as well as with supplication. Believe that I am with you and that I care.

I will give you a peace that runs deeper than your deepest problem. I will help you keep your heart in my Son Jesus. He will be there long after the problem is gone.

Think about other things. In the world, you can find honorable acts, lovely sights, justice-seeking people, sunrises, music. Put these things in your mind and rejoice in them.

You cannot worry and rejoice at the very same time. Rejoice a little.

We respond to God.

- We are weighed down with a problem. We may want to tell God about it and let ourselves feel unburdened. In that prayer, we can rejoice that God is present—really present.
- We see only the dark side of our concern. We may want to ask for the grace to fill our mind with the good things in the world.
- We seek peace. We may want to make a deep-breathing prayer, breathing out our tension, breathing in the peace that only God gives.

We are taught to work, but few of us learn to rest. We grow up with adages: "Idleness is the devil's workshop." "The early bird catches the worm." "Busy hands, fat purse."

Work is good. Too much work can be distracting (keeping us from reflection) and distancing (keeping us from intimacy).

Rest provides a holy balance.

Recreation re-creates. Sleeping late restores. Meditating and thinking clarifies. Conversing and playing unifies. These are ways to rest. To rest is to imitate God.

Exodus 20:8–11

Remember the sabbath day, to keep it holy. Six days you shall labor, and do all your work; but the seventh day is a sabbath to the Lord your God; in it you shall not do any work, you, or your son, or your daughter, your man-servant, or your maid-servant, or your cattle, or the sojourner who is within your gates; for in six days the Lord made heaven and earth, the sea, and all that is in them, and rested the seventh day; therefore the Lord blessed the sabbath day and hallowed it.

The Dialogue

We listen to God speak.

Sabbath is not something that happened when I stopped creating. I *created* sabbath. I first made light, later plants and animals, then humankind—and I ended creation by creating blessed rest—the sabbath.

Rest, like sunshine and trees, is my created gift to you.

Rest is also my command to you. It's that important.

Rest is holy because to rest is to imitate me.

Teach your sons and daughters to keep this good commandment.

We respond to God.
- We have much responsibility. We hear this passage as a call to change by relaxing more. We may want to pray for creative ideas to help us find and take some five-minute leisures during the day.
- We keep ourselves too busy. We may need to ask forgiveness for giving too much time to projects and not enough to people (including ourselves).
- We teach our sons and daughters the value of hard work because work is a value to us. We may ask God to help us enlarge our own value to include leisure and to pass that enlarged value on to our children.
- We enjoy late sleeping or quiet thinking or bird watching or other leisures. We may want to thank God for this good gift of rest.

LETTING GO OF CHILDREN

When little children stand alone for the first time and take their first unaided step, they are making a symbolic beginning of their journey away from their parents and toward independence. It's an instinctive journey, so deeply imbedded in the human psyche that it is nearly impossible to curb it.

That first independent step sets off a kind of tug of war between parents and children. Parents set limits; children struggle against limits. Usually the battle is fairly subtle and civilized; occasionally it's almost brutal. But it must be waged in each generation.

Parents worry. If only their children would wait until they have enough sense, enough experience and skill, enough will power—if only they would wait until they are prepared to meet the world.

Children seldom wait.

John 17:11–18

And now I am no more in the world, but they are in the world, and I am coming to thee. Holy Father, keep them in thy name, which thou hast given me, that they may be one, even as we are one. While I was with them, I kept them in thy name, which thou hast given me; I have guarded them, and none of them is lost but the son of perdition, that the scripture might be fulfilled. But now I am coming to thee; and these things I speak in the world, that they may have my joy fulfilled in themselves. I have given them thy word; and the world has hated them because they are not of the world, even as I am not of the world. I do not pray that thou shouldst take them out of the world, but that thou shouldst keep them from the evil one. They are not of the world, even as I am not of the world. Sanctify them in the truth; thy

word is truth. As thou didst send me into the world, so
I have sent them into the world.

The Dialogue

We listen to God speak.

Death is just around the corner for my Son Jesus. He is
coming home. He is leaving his disciples—no, he is *sending*
them out into the world.

They are not yet spiritually mature. In fact, Peter (the
"rock") will be slow to understand his task. He will quarrel
with Paul about the Gentiles.

They are not ready. But my Son leaves them. He lets
them go.

Despite my Son's love, one of them is "lost."

Your children, like Jesus' disciples, will make choices—
and mistakes.

Pray for them. Pray, as Jesus prayed, that they will be
sanctified in truth.

I will protect them with my name. My name is God.
Truth.

We respond to God.
- We worry about a particular child. We may need to pray for
  our child to be protected by God's name.
- We are aware of our children's growth in independence. We
  may want to thank God for that.
- We feel afraid of not being needed. Consequently, we are pos-
  sessive of our children. We hear this passage as a call to grow
  by letting go. We may want to talk about that with the Lord.

PRAYING FOR SOMEONE

We pray for people we love. Sometimes we pray out of a sense of powerlessness: we have no power to relieve job pressures for a spouse or to make a son or daughter more popular at school or to make a sick person well or a sad person happy. We have no power. So we pray.

Sometimes love inspires us to pray. In our affection, we want to give personal gifts such as smiles, touching, listening. Prayer can be one of these gifts.

Sometimes we simply pray a blessing.

Numbers 6:22–27

The Lord said to Moses, "Say to Aaron and his sons, 'Thus you shall bless the people of Israel: you shall say to them, The Lord bless you and keep you: The Lord make his face to shine upon you, and be gracious to you: The Lord lift up his countenance upon you, and give you peace.' So shall they put my name upon the people of Israel, and I will bless them."

The Dialogue

We listen to God speak.

I gave some very powerful words to those two ancestors of yours, Moses and Aaron. The words are still powerful. Use them.

Like Moses and Aaron, you can cause my face to shine on people. In biblical language, *face* represents *disposition.* A shining face means a gracious disposition.

You can use these blessing words to call my graciousness on your spouse, your children, your friends.

They are my people. Put my name on them.
I will bless them.

We respond to God.
- We are inclined to give God detailed descriptions of how we want him to help people we love. We may decide to trust more that God will bless them in his wisdom, and we pray for deepened trust.
- We have a habit of praying for people only when we worry about them. We may resolve to say this scriptural blessing regularly for the people we love.
- We realize that many people have brought God's blessing on us through prayer. Parents, friends, spouses, pastors: many have caused God's face to shine on us. We thank God for those people and also for God himself.

Company is coming. We straighten up the house a little. If it's someone extra special, we really get with it, cleaning, cooking, mowing, and spraying a little clean-smelling Pine Sol into the corners.

A family, in the nuclear sense, is a couple or a group of people bonded together by blood or law and, hopefully, by affection. Families tend to wrap walls around themselves—houses, apartments, or tents. These physical boundaries with family members inside and non-family persons outside represent the psycho-social identity of the family as a semi-private group. People who are not family members are not supposed to pass through those boundaries without the welcome of the family.

Having company means that people open the boundaries and share the people inside the walls.

It's a fun and holy thing for families to do—healthy, too.

Genesis 18:1–8
And the Lord appeared to him by the oaks of Mamre, as he sat at the door of his tent in the heat of the day. He lifted up his eyes and looked, and behold, three men stood in front of him. When he saw them, he ran from the tent door to meet them, and bowed himself to the earth, and said, "My lord, if I have found favor in your sight, do not pass by your servant. Let a little water be brought, and wash your feet, and rest yourselves under the tree, while I fetch a morsel of bread, that you may refresh yourselves, and after that you may pass on—since you have come to your servant." So they said, "Do as you have said." And Abraham hastened into the tent to Sarah, and said, "Make ready quickly three measures of fine meal, knead it, and make cakes." And Abraham ran to the herd, and took a

calf, tender and good, and gave it to the servant, who hastened to prepare it. Then he took curds, and milk, and the
calf which he had prepared, and set it before them; and he
stood by them under the tree while they ate.

The Dialogue

We listen to God speak.

This story about one of my most likable sons, Abraham,
is set in a time and place (close to four thousand years ago in
the Sinai desert) that considered hospitality as one of the essential laws of the desert.

In the first sentence, I make it clear that I am the guest.
Don't be confused by the three men. I come in many forms.

Notice how Abraham *ran* to meet us, *fetched* bread, *hastened* to tell about our presence, and gave orders to *make
ready quickly.* And all that, mind you, in the heat of the day,
in the desert, for "strangers." He was energetic. He was generous.

I like that.

Hospitality is a virtue that welcomes people in. It en-
larges families. It recognizes that all people belong to one family—mine.

I like you to be welcoming the way Abraham was. When
you do, you welcome me.

We respond to God.
- We are a somewhat isolated family. We feel embarrassed
  about our home or awkward around non-family persons. In
  this passage, we may hear God call us to become more open
  and to risk inviting someone into our home.
- We enjoy having company. We may want to thank God for
  this gift of hospitality and for his presence in our guests.

• Some people barge in on us too often. We may want to talk with God about our feelings and ask for wisdom in deciding how to keep a balance between family privacy and hospitality.

PUTTING UP WITH DIFFERENCES

If uniqueness is a gift, it is often also a trial, because to be unique means to be different. We can be different from others in our values, beliefs, temperaments, tastes, habits, backgrounds, and numerous other ways.

We experience differences only in relation to other people. One chews with his mouth open; another speaks in tongues, for goodness' sake; someone else talks too loud; others are shy, black, white, rich, emotional. When we experience others as different from ourselves in these human ways, our tendency may be to judge them as being wrong or bad.

On the other hand, some of us tend to note how we differ from others and immediately judge that we are the ones who are wrong or bad.

Our task is to accept human differences not as wrong or bad, but simply as different.

Ephesians 4:1–6

I therefore, a prisoner for the Lord, beg you to lead a life worthy of the calling to which you have been called, with all lowliness and meekness, with patience, forbearing one another in love, eager to maintain the unity of the Spirit in the bond of peace. There is one body and one Spirit, just as you were called to the one hope that belongs to your call, one Lord, one faith, one baptism, one God and Father of us all, who is above all and through all and in all.

The Dialogue

We listen to God speak.

My good friend Paul is speaking my word to you from prison.

You have received a "calling" from me. It may be a call to marriage, to parenthood, to a ministry or a job. My call to you puts you in relationship with others. Be patient with them.

Try hard. Put up with one another in love. Be eager to keep unity.

If you are unified, you will be bound together in peace. My Spirit is the source of unity.

There are lots of things different between you and other believing persons, but just look at the things that are the same—the same hope; the same faith; the same me!

I am the God and Father of all of you.

I am God *in* all of you.

We respond to God.

- We feel very irritated by a "different" habit or temperament of someone in our family. We may want to ask the Holy Spirit to help us diminish our irritation and grow in patience.
- We cannot understand how God lives in everyone, but we believe he does. We feel bonded to others. We may want to reflect with praise on this terrific mystery.
- We believe God calls us to this marriage, this family, this neighborhood. He gives us the opportunity to bring his unity into a tiny part of the world. We may want to thank God for our calling.
- We believe the Holy Spirit continually moves people toward harmony, peace, unity. We see how ecumenism is a larger expression of unity in a marriage, and we are aware that we have sometimes hampered religious unity by our prejudice or smugness. We may want to ask forgiveness for setting back God's plan.

Here we have this child, a new human being. The world has held many people, but it has never before held her. She is unique; that is, she is unrepeated and unrepeatable.

We give her a name so she can identify herself in the world. When people ask "Who are you?" she will answer with the name we now give. "I am Louise."

In the Bible, naming is a very serious business. It is important that a name "fit"—so important that names are changed when a person's character or role changes: Abram to Abraham, Saul to Paul, Jacob to Israel, Peter to Rock.

We want to give this child a name that fits. We helped create her from our own bodies. Now, in another holy, creative act, we give her her name.

Luke 2:15–21

When the angels went away from them into heaven, the shepherds said to one another, "Let us go over to Bethlehem and see this thing that has happened, which the Lord has made known to us." And they went with haste, and found Mary and Joseph, and the babe lying in a manger. And when they saw it they made known the saying which had been told them concerning this child; and all who heard it wondered at what the shepherds told them. But Mary kept all these things, pondering them in her heart. And the shepherds returned, glorifying and praising God for all they had heard and seen, as it had been told them.

And at the end of eight days, when he was circumcised, he was called Jesus, the name given by the angel before he was conceived in the womb.

The Dialogue

We listen to God speak.

I know this Child, my Son, and I give him a name that fits. On earth, his name is *Jesus* which means *Savior*. He is named that because he saves.

I also know your child. I knew her before she was conceived.

Ponder in your heart, as Mary did, all that you know. Choose her name carefully.

We respond to God.

- We are aware that it is our joyful and serious task to give this new person a name to carry in the world. We may want to pray that the name we give will "fit" and that the child will bear it with simple pride.
- We are awed by the uniqueness of our child and by the fact that God knew her even before she was conceived. We may want to praise God for the mystery of her life.
- We realize that, in the biblical sense, to name means to know. We pray that we will really know this child.

Our feet hurt, our backs ache, our shoulders slump, our eyelids droop. This business of family living is hard work. We get so tired.

We decide to snatch forty winks, and the phone rings. We plan to soak in a tub of warm water with a book, and a child vomits. We look forward to kicking off our shoes when we get home after work, and find unwashed dishes and unmowed lawns. A spouse needs to talk. A child needs to cry. A neighbor needs a ride.

Sometimes the work seems never-ending.

This wasn't what we had in mind when, years ago, we stood, beaming and nervous, reciting marriage vows.

Mark 6:30–34

The apostles returned to Jesus, and told him all that they had done and taught. And he said to them, "Come away by yourselves to a lonely place, and rest a while." For many were coming and going, and they had no leisure even to eat. And they went away in the boat to a lonely place by themselves. Now many saw them going, and knew them, and they ran there on foot from all the towns, and got there ahead of them. As he landed he saw a great throng, and he had compassion on them, because they were like sheep without a shepherd; and he began to teach them many things.

The Dialogue

We listen to God speak.

John the Baptizer has just been murdered for preaching my call to repentance and conversion. Preaching is dangerous.

77

So the apostles are tired as much from tension as from their hard work of preaching that same message.

My Son Jesus plans a little respite for himself and those tired apostles.

Even though he is tired, Jesus finds enough energy to preach to the people. He finds the energy in compassion. Compassion means a lively desire to help another.

Apostle means one who is sent out. You are sent out, too. I send you to this spouse, this family. It takes a lot of work, this being sent out.

Sometimes you will need to rest, and that is just fine. After all, I created the sabbath.

But sometimes people around you may need you in various ways, and you may have to seek energy in compassion.

We respond to God.
- We work hard and feel tired. We also feel unappreciated and resentful. In God's word, we hear a call to change by growing in compassion for those we live with. We may pray that God will deepen our compassion.
- We realize that we really are "sent out" and that our apostleship as couples is to help create loving families. We know this is important both for the family members and for the world. We may thank God for calling us to this good work.
- We see our spouses under much strain. We want to call them to "a lonely place" to rest. We may thank God for their compassion and ask God to help them take the rest they need.

If we have lived very long at all, the odds are good that we have spent some time in the awful desert of discouragement.

We try hard, and things don't turn out. We have a dream, and it crumbles at our feet. We set out in a certain direction in life, and the road becomes impassable. We build up a career, and lose it.

When we are deeply discouraged, nothing seems to help. So we enter the desert. In extreme cases, we may even wish we could die.

1 Kings 19:4–8

> But he himself went a day's journey into the wilderness, and came and sat down under a broom tree; and he asked that he might die, saying "It is enough; now, O Lord, take away my life; for I am no better than my fathers." And he lay down and slept under a broom tree; and behold, an angel touched him, and said to him, "Arise and eat." And he looked, and behold, there was at his head a cake baked on hot stones and a jar of water. And he ate and drank, and lay down again. And the angel of the Lord came again a second time, and touched him, and said, "Arise and eat, else the journey will be too great for you." And he arose, and ate and drank, and went in the strength of that food forty days and forty nights to Horeb the mount of God.

The Dialogue

We listen to God speak.

Shortly before this, Elijah dramatically showed that I alone am God and that Baal is powerless. Queen Jezebel was upset that her god Baal looked so impotent. Now she is seeking to have Elijah killed. Elijah, wisely, is hiding out. Sweet success turns to bitter disappointment.

You have had that kind of turning experience.

I offer Elijah plain bread and water. It's more than food. It's a call to hope again. He needs the strength of that bread and water. After all, he is walking to my mountain.

I want you to know that I offer you, too, the bread and water of strong hope.

You, too, are on your way to the mountain of God.

We respond to God.

- We feel discouraged. Sometimes we almost wish we were dead because life holds too much pain. In this passage, we hear God call us to return to hope. We may pray that we will eat the Lord's food and find strength again.
- We realize we are on a long journey which leads to the mountain of God, heaven. Believing that, we feel strengthened. We may praise God and thank him for giving us this great destination and the strength to keep to the road.
- We know someone who is presently discouraged. We take a moment to consider how that person may be feeling. We ask God to help us find some way to carry bread and water to that person.

HAVING A CHILD BAPTIZED

"Our whence determines our whither," says the Bible professor. Our whence is where we have come from; our whither is where we are going to. Baptism means that God is both our whence and our whither.

When we present this child for baptism, we are setting him on a clear road, a road that begins with God and ends with God. Is there any better thing we could do for this child?

God receives our child—not because of the child's faith or our virtue, but because God is good.

Titus 3:4–8a

But when the goodness and loving kindness of God our Savior appeared, he saved us, not because of deeds done by us in righteousness, but in virtue of his own mercy, by the washing of regeneration and renewal in the Holy Spirit, which he poured out upon us richly through Jesus Christ our Savior, so that we might be justified by his grace and become heirs in hope of eternal life. The saying is sure.

The Dialogue

We listen to God speak.

Notice that there is no arithmetic in my relationship with you—nothing like: you do so many righteous deeds and then I'll even things out by giving you baptism. No, I give baptism to you (and to your child) because I am good.

Notice the generosity in these words inspired by me for you. I "pour" out regeneration. I do it "richly."

Your child is going to live forever! So are you. That's what I mean by "eternal life."

This saying is sure.

We respond to God.

- This child, so new on Planet Earth, is going to live on and on and on—forever. This child is abundantly loved. We may want to reflect on this beyond-imagination fact. We may want to make our total response one of awe and praise and thanks.

- We want our child not only to *be* so loved but also to *know* he is loved so much by our generous God. We may want to respond with a petition for wisdom in parenting.

One thing that influences our choices of marriage partners is plain old sexual attraction.

Like other intimate acts, love-making can hold various messages. Sometimes it is an act of pure play. Sometimes it may be part of an apology. Sometimes it is a tender way to comfort. Occasionally it might be an act of wild passion.

Just as some couples find it hard to communicate verbally, some find it hard to communicate sexually. In either case, it would be wise to seek help.

God gives us both languages—words and sex—as special gifts of intimacy. When those two languages come together in love-making, we "make" love. And God is pleased.

Genesis 2:18–24

Then the Lord God said, "It is not good that the man should be alone; I will make him a helper fit for him." So out of the ground the Lord God formed every beast of the field and every bird of the air, and brought them to the man to see what he would call them; and whatever the man called every living creature, that was its name. The man gave names to all cattle, and to the birds of the air, and to every beast of the field; but for the man there was not found a helper fit for him. So the Lord God caused a deep sleep to fall upon the man, and while he slept took one of his ribs and closed up its place with flesh; and the rib which the Lord God had taken from the man he made into a woman and brought her to the man. Then the man said

"This at last is bone of my bones
and flesh of my flesh;
she shall be called Woman,
because she was taken out of Man."

Therefore a man leaves his father and his mother and cleaves to his wife, and they become one flesh. And the man and his wife were both naked, and were not ashamed.

The Dialogue

We listen to God speak.

These words of mine come early in the Scripture because they are basic to understanding who I am to you and who you are to one another. In fact, I repeat them three times in the Bible.

Isolation is not good for people. I gave you a social nature. Marriage is a special expression of that social instinct.

This is a story about the first marriage. If you translate into your own idiom what Adam says when he sees his bride, it will be something like this: "What a stroke of good luck! Just what I was wanting." I put that wanting inside you too.

In my plan, the marriage bond is even stronger than the parent-child bond. Don't let anyone—not even your parents—take precedence over your spouse.

One thing more: when I speak of unashamed nakedness, I'm speaking of intimacy. Enjoy.

We respond to God.

- We enjoy love-making and are aware of its various qualities of tenderness, playfulness, solace. We may respond to God's word with thanksgiving for such a lovely, earthy gift.
- We do not enjoy sexual intimacy as fully or as freely as we would like. We may respond to God by talking honestly about our feelings and asking for courage to seek better ways to accept this gift.
- We find ourselves hung-up on getting approval from our parents and on keeping in too close touch with them. Our spouses resent this. We may want to pray for the courage

and grown-upness to put our spouses in first place, according to God's plan.

- We want to teach our children the natural goodness of sex. We may ask God to bless them with healthy attitudes about sexual love in marriage.

When couples first experience the exhilaration of their love for one another, they sometimes wish they could build themselves a house to keep the world out and their love in. But love would die.

To *be* loved carries the responsibility to *give* love.

By its nature, love is generous. It overflows. It keeps manufacturing itself.

Hopefully we keep the exhilaration. Hopefully we also discover that mature love means reaching out beyond ourselves with esteem for others and active caring.

Reaching out can make us happier and can also enrich our own families.

Acts 10:34–38

And Peter opened his mouth and said: "Truly I perceive that God shows no partiality, but in every nation any one who fears him and does what is right is acceptable to him. You know the word which he sent to Israel, preaching good news of peace by Jesus Christ (he is Lord of all), the word which was proclaimed throughout all Judea, beginning from Galilee after the baptism which John preached: how God anointed Jesus of Nazareth with the Holy Spirit and with power; how he went about doing good and healing all that were oppressed by the devil, for God was with him."

The Dialogue

We listen to God speak.

I show no partiality. Literally, that means I don't judge by faces—that is, by appearances.

I accept all people who fear me. *To fear* means *to be in right relationship.* Our relationship is that of God to son and daughter, Creator to creature. When you live rightly in that relationship, I accept you.

As soon as Jesus was baptized, he went about doing good. I was with him.

Jesus did good by preaching the good news and by healing hearts and bodies.

You are baptized, too—anointed by me, filled with the same Holy Spirit.

Go about doing good.

I am with you.

We respond to God.

- We see so many needs in our marriage and in our families as well as in the rest of the world. We cannot do it all. We pray for wisdom to spend our energies wisely, balancing service with self-care.
- We find a way to reach out helpfully. We may want to talk with God about this work and thank him for this opportunity to imitate Jesus.
- We need some help ourselves. We may want to pray for direction in seeking help and thank God for the chance to receive as well as to give.
- We tend to judge by people's faces, to "show partiality" by trying to determine who "deserves" help. We hear this passage as a call to let go of pre-judgment. We may want to ask God to help us imitate him by giving up our partiality.

ADJUSTING DREAMS

When couples decide to marry, they begin to fashion dreams—dreams about how they'll love and be loved; about status and position; about income, job, and home; about children. It's highly unlikely one person's dreams will exactly correspond to the partner's dreams. It's even less likely that all the dreams will become reality.

One task of marriage is to infuse reality with vision while adjusting dreams to reality.

Exodus 17:3–7

> But the people thirsted there for water, and they murmured against Moses, and said, "Why did you bring us up out of Egypt, to kill us and our children and our cattle with thirst?" So Moses cried to the Lord, "What shall I do with this people? They are almost ready to stone me." And the Lord said to Moses, "Pass on before the people, taking with you some of the elders of Israel; and take in your hand the rod with which you struck the Nile, and go. Behold, I will stand before you there on the rock of Horeb; and you shall strike the rock, and water shall come out of it, that the people may drink. And Moses did so, in the sight of the elders of Israel. And he called the name of the place Massah and Meribah, because of the fault-finding of the children of Israel, and because they put the Lord to the proof by saying, "Is the Lord among us, or not?"

The Dialogue

We listen to God speak.

When my people left hated Egypt, they carried dreams of milk and honey. The desert thirst did not correspond to their dream.

I listen to and instruct those who pray to me—even when the prayer is a complaint.

I can bring water even out of desert rock.

They/you ask, "Is the Lord among us or not?" Yes, I am among you. Then. Now. Always.

My dream for you may not match your dream for yourself, but know that I am among you. That's the greatest dream—and reality.

We respond to God.
- Another dream has been broken. We may want to talk with the Lord about that.
- Our faith is faltering. We don't clearly experience the presence of God. We may want to ask for reassurance that God is here with us.
- We are sad about a lost dream, but we firmly believe that, no matter what, God is here with us. We may want simply to praise and thank God.

FRETTING ABOUT THE KIDS

"Why have you done this to us?" This is a fretful cry of parents which rings through the ages. Even Jesus' earth parents uttered the cry.

We fret because we fear. What if our kids are unhappy? Unpopular? Sick? Immoral?

We fret because we are helpless. We would give our life-blood if, by that, we could let them experience life fully and, at the same time, protect them from mistakes and pain.

We fret because we don't understand. Theirs is a different world, and we don't understand it. Actually we don't fully understand these unique persons, our kids.

We fret because we love.

Worrying seems to be part of the universal parent-task. To a degree, it's good and necessary. Beyond that degree, it may be damaging to both our kids and ourselves.

Luke 2:41–50

Now his parents went to Jerusalem every year at the feast of the Passover. And when he was twelve years old, they went up according to custom; and when the feast was ended, as they were returning, the boy Jesus stayed behind in Jerusalem. His parents did not know it, but supposing him to be in the company they went a day's journey, and they sought him among their kinsfolk and acquaintances; and when they did not find him, they returned to Jerusalem, seeking him.

After three days they found him in the temple, sitting among the teachers, listening to them and asking them questions; and all who heard him were amazed at his understanding and his answers. And when they saw him they were astonished; and his mother said to him, "Son, why have you treated us so? Behold, your father and I have been looking for you anxiously." And he said to them, "How is it that you sought me? Did you not know that I must be in my Father's house?" And they did not understand the saying which he spoke to them.

The Dialogue

We listen to God speak.

This is the only biblical passage I have given you about Jesus' boyhood. It holds important teachings. One teaching is that children will move into life in ways that often bewilder parents.

Mary is upset. First of all, Jesus is lost. (Lost to her, that is; he feels quite at home in "my Father's house.") Second, even after she and Joseph find Jesus, she doesn't understand. Not understanding is troubling.

I do not give Mary and Joseph explanations. I don't give you explanations either.

Your children are my daughters and sons. We have our own relationship. I may call them in a way you do not understand.

We respond to God.

● We believe that God has a personal relationship with us, and we begin to understand more clearly that God also really does have personal relationships with our kids. We may want to respond to God's word about this mystery with genuine thanks.

● We are worried about one of our kids. We may want to talk to God the Father about our concerns and make petitions for help.

● We realize that we worry too much, and perhaps nag or worry our kids too much. We may hear this passage as a call to change by growing in trust. We talk this over humbly with God and ask for his help in this change.

- One of our kids has bitterly disappointed us. We alternately blame her or blame ourselves. We think we didn't emphasize the right values. We think she refused to learn from us. We may give this past history to God, who is after all the Lord of history. We ask for forgiveness and receive peace.

One of the unsettling things about marriage is that we are found out! Our spouses learn, first-hand, that we are not perfect.

Our morning breath is asphyxiating. We are moody. We pinch pennies. Tardiness is a habit. Our chests are too flat. We are untidy.

For some of us, being imperfect is almost intolerable. We are more apt to be defensive about our humanness if our spouses expect us to be perfect—or if we think that's what they expect.

Actually, one of the redeeming graces of marriage should be that we are known as we really are and that we are nevertheless loved. And we can extend that same graceful acceptance to another imperfect and lovable person.

Exodus 4:10–17

But Moses said to the Lord, "Oh, my Lord, I am not eloquent, either heretofore or since thou hast spoken to thy servant; but I am slow of speech and of tongue." Then the Lord said to him, "Who has made man's mouth? Who makes him dumb, or deaf, or seeing, or blind? Is it not I, the Lord? Now therefore go, and I will be with your mouth and teach you what you shall speak." But he said, "Oh, my Lord, send, I pray, some other person." Then the anger of the Lord was kindled against Moses and he said, "Is there not Aaron, your brother, the Levite? I know that he can speak well; and behold, he is coming out to meet you, and when he sees you he will be glad in his heart. And you shall speak to him and put the words in his mouth; and I will be with your mouth and with his mouth, and will teach you what you shall do. He shall speak for you to the people; and he shall be a mouth for you, and

you shall be to him as God. And you shall take in your
hand this rod, with which you shall do the signs."

The Dialogue

We listen to God speak.

It's true that I love Moses very much and that the job I've
given him is difficult. But the way he hesitates by putting himself down angers me. First he says "Who am I?"—as if he were
a nobody! Now he says he isn't eloquent—as if I choose only
the perfect to work for justice!

I have given you a difficult job, too: to work for peace and
justice in your family and beyond it. In a way, the job is too
big for you because you are not perfect. You are human.

But remember this: I will be in your mouth and teach you
what you shall speak. Moses—stammering Moses—is my
promise.

We respond to God.

- We recognize imperfections in our spouses and we also love
  them. We believe our love is redeeming, the way God's love
  is for us. We may thank God for this chance to imitate him
  by loving our very human spouse.
- In many ways, we fall short in our spouses' eyes or in our own.
  We try to defend ourselves by withdrawing or blaming or kow-
  towing. These behaviors keep us from accepting our own humanity. We may ask God for help in being more real, more
  humble.
- We believe that today we benefit from the work Moses did
  centuries ago and from the work of other imperfect people
  who have sought justice in the world. We thank God for this
  heritage.

MAKING UP

After a quarrel, if the marriage is to continue with unity and joy, we have to make up with each other.

Making up does not mean to dog-bone an issue, temporarily burying it with the full intention of digging it back up.

To make up means to make good again—to come to terms, to reconcile.

It's important for us to learn to resolve issues in a way that leaves both of us winners. It's important for us to listen to our spouses' viewpoints enough to compromise. It's important for us to put our arms around one another.

Genesis 33:1–4

And Jacob lifted up his eyes and looked, and behold, Esau was coming, and four hundred men with him. So he divided the children among Leah and Rachel and the two maids. And he put the maids with their children in front, then Leah with her children, and Rachel and Joseph last of all. He himself went on before them, bowing himself to the ground seven times, until he came near to his brother.

But Esau ran to meet him, and embraced him, and fell on his neck and kissed him, and they wept.

The Dialogue

We listen to God speak.

These two roguish twins started fighting in the womb and the struggle went on until finally Jacob stole Esau's birthright. Esau was murderously angry and Jacob fled the country. The event in this passage takes place years later.

All those years of anger and separation end with an embrace.

This story pattern is repeated many times in my word. My people become faithless, and I become angry. Then I send prophets. I pick them up in my arms again.

My Son tells a story with the same pattern, a story about a father and his prodigal son.

These stories all end with embraces.

We respond to God.
- We quarrel a lot with our spouses. In this passage, we hear God calling us to find new ways to be more unified, perhaps through counseling, communication workshops, or marriage enrichment programs. We may talk with God about this call to grow and about our feelings.
- We are aware that our spouses help maintain unity in our marriage by their willingness to make up quickly after a quarrel. We recognize that this habit is a reflection in them of God's reconciliation with us. We may thank God and hug our spouse.
- Our children are people, too. They are learning now how to relate in marriage by seeing how their parents relate to each other and to them. We may ask God to help us make up with our children and to help them grow up to be generous in reconciliation.

Making ends meet takes some juggling as well as some money, and even then the ends sometimes don't meet.

Money-related issues are among the stickiest issues in marriage. Usually the real problem is not how much money is available but how the available money is managed.

One is a saver, the other a spender. One is a bargain-hunter, the other an impulsive buyer. One is a credit card user, the other a cash carrier.

Balancing a budget often boils down to compromising.

For Christians, balancing a budget is also an expression of values.

Matthew 22:15–22

Then the Pharisees went and took counsel how to entangle him in his talk. And they sent their disciples to him, along with the Herodians, saying, "Teacher, we know that you are true, and teach the way of God truthfully, and care for no man; for you do not regard the position of men. Tell us, then, what you think. Is it lawful to pay taxes to Caesar, or not?" But Jesus, aware of their malice, said, "Why put me to the test, you hypocrites? Show me the money for the tax." And they brought him a coin. And Jesus said to them, "Whose likeness and inscription is this?" They said, "Caesar's." Then he said to them, "Render therefore to Caesar the things that are Caesar's, and to God the things that are God's." When they heard it, they marveled; and they left him and went away.

The Dialogue

We listen to God speak.

The Pharisees have set this scene up as a Catch-22 situation. They oppose paying taxes to the Romans. The Herodians support Roman rule. The Pharisees figure that Jesus will be in trouble with one group or the other by whichever way he answers.

My Son's reply is not just a side-stepping answer to a trick question. It is a straight answer rooted in justice.

Jesus does not intend to divide the world into Caesar's part and my part. He intends people to live in a just way and sometimes you will experience tension in sorting this out.

His answer stands for you—today.

We respond to God.
- We have enough money and feel satisfied with the way we render to Caesar and render to God. We may thank God for helping us achieve unity in this area.
- Our contributions to the church are minimal and irregular. We realize that we take services for granted as part of our due for attending church. We may talk this over with God. We may respond by making a commitment to contribute more regularly to the church or to groups that work for justice.
- We spend more than we make and end up not paying our bills. In these words of Scripture, we may hear God call us to learn new ways of managing money, perhaps by getting professional help from certain banks or from counseling.

EATING OUT (OR IN)

Friends drop by, so we set out some peanuts and beer. Relatives are coming, so we splurge on shrimp. A child turns four, so we bake a cake. A neighbor dies, so we take a ham to the grieving family.

When people gather in affection, they nearly always break bread in one form or another. Eating together is a sign of welcome and friendship. For Christians, eating together becomes an opportunity to recognize God in our midst. This is true whether the meal takes place in the cathedral or in the back yard.

John 21:9–14

When they got out on land, they saw a charcoal fire there, with fish lying on it, and bread. Jesus said to them, "Bring some of the fish that you have just caught." So Simon Peter went aboard and hauled the net ashore, full of large fish, a hundred and fifty-three of them; and although there were so many, the net was not torn. Jesus said to them, "Come and have breakfast." Now none of the disciples dared ask him, "Who are you?" They knew it was the Lord. Jesus came and took the bread and gave it to them, and so with the fish. This was now the third time that Jesus was revealed to the disciples after he was raised from the dead.

The Dialogue

We listen to God speak.

My Son Jesus lives again! It is important for the disciples to know that his resurrection is real and not just some fanciful fantasy of theirs. Jesus has a cookout for them—fish fry.

This act of eating has meaning on two levels. On one level, it is an assurance of Jesus' aliveness in the world. On another level it is a symbol of the Eucharist.

My Son Jesus makes himself food for you in the Eucharist. He still lives!

When you eat with friends, I also am there.

We respond to God.

- We become tense when relatives or friends come to our home for a meal. Our nervousness diminishes our ability to enjoy and appreciate our visitors. We may ask God to help us relax and welcome our guests more naturally.

- We enjoy eating whether with our spouses alone or with others. We like not only the taste of food but also the laughter and the story swapping and the togetherness. We may thank God for the sensual pleasure of taste and for the warmth of companionship.

- We often take communion or share other meals without much awareness that Jesus really is present. When eating with our spouses, we may be taciturn or distracted or grumpy. Meals are not pleasant times. We may talk about these habits and ask God to help us deepen our awareness of his presence.

If we live very long at all, we will experience grief. Serious sickness, death, alcoholism, job loss: these experiences bring grief.

Grief is a whole bundle of emotions, including rage, despair, and sadness. These emotions pound within us during sleepless nights and hopeless days.

Sometimes all these feelings become even more complicated because we feel guilty about grieving itself—guilty about our rage, especially. We forget, or perhaps haven't yet learned, that the expression of rage can be a healthy way to vent our feelings.

God gives us models in Scripture.

Job 7:1–6; 42:7–8

Has not man a hard service upon earth
 and are not his days like the days of a hireling?
Like a slave who longs for the shadow,
 and like a hireling who looks for his wages,
So I am allotted months of emptiness,
 and nights of misery are apportioned to me.
When I lie down I say, "When shall I arise?"
 But the night is long,
 and I am full of tossing till the dawn.
My flesh is clothed with worms and dirt;
 my skin hardens, then breaks off afresh.
My days are swifter than a weaver's shuttle,
 and come to their end without hope.

· · · · ·

After the Lord had spoken these words to Job, the Lord said to Eliphaz the Temanite: "My wrath is kindled against

you and against your two friends; for you have not spoken
of me what is right, as my servant Job has. Now therefore
take seven bulls and seven rams, and go to my servant Job,
and offer up for yourselves a burnt offering; and my servant Job shall pray for you, for I will accept his prayer not
to deal with you according to your folly; for you have not
spoken of me what is right, as my servant Job has."

The Dialogue

We listen to God speak.

Job doesn't mince words. He curses his life. He comes
close to cursing me. He rants and raves.

Job's "friends," on the other hand, advise, accuse, analyze, and sermonize.

I do not like what the friends say. I like what Job says. He
uses words that match what is in his heart.

You have times in your life when you feel the way Job
feels.

Tell me about it.

We respond to God.

- We feel angry toward God because our suffering doesn't
  seem fair. Besides our own suffering, there is pain all over
  the world. We wonder why people, especially little children, have to suffer so much. We may speak our anger and
  our sadness.

- Friends are grief-stricken and we don't know what to say to
  them. We may ask God to help us find a few true words and
  to be with our friends in quiet love.

- In this passage, we recognize more clearly that we can speak
  our hearts to God. He doesn't want flowery words when our
  hearts are full of need. We may thank God for the security
  we feel in revealing our deepest selves to him. What a
  friend!

PLANNING THE FUTURE

Two mental faculties—memory and fantasy—enable us to experience various time zones. Memory keeps the past available. Fantasy plans the future.

It all comes together in the now. We are the person we are today partly because of choices we made yesterday and partly because of dreams we have for tomorrow.

We know we can't do much about the past, but we persist in thinking we can take charge of the future. To some extent, we can.

1 Peter 1:17–25

And if you invoke as Father him who judges each one impartially according to his deeds, conduct yourselves with fear throughout the time of your exile. You know that you were ransomed from the futile ways inherited from your fathers, not with perishable things such as silver or gold, but with the precious blood of Christ, like that of a lamb without blemish or spot. He was destined before the foundation of the world but was made manifest at the end of the times for your sake. Through him you have confidence in God, who raised him from the dead and gave him glory, so that your faith and hope are in God. Having purified your souls by your obedience to the truth for a sincere love of the brethren, love one another earnestly from the heart. You have been born anew, not of perishable seed but of imperishable, through the living and abiding word of God; for

"All flesh is like grass
and all its glory like the flower of grass.
The grass withers, and the flower falls,
but the word of the Lord abides for ever."

That word is the good news which was preached to you.

The Dialogue

We listen to God speak.

Peter is addressing the Jews in exile. The words are also for you. In a way, you are in exile until you come home.

After all, you belong to me. I have ransomed you with the very blood of Jesus. That's a dear price. See how important you are to me.

You are going to live forever.

That is your destiny.

That is the good news!

We respond to God.

- We spend energy preparing for the future with IRAs, insurance policies, investments, and wills. And all the time, there is an itching thought inside us—the knowledge that there is no foolproof system. We may do what seems sensible and ask God to help us trust in him.
- We may keep ourselves preoccupied with our earthly future and forget the final future which is life with God—forever. We may ask for deeper faith.
- We are all on our way to the mountain of God. We may rejoice in this destiny which exceeds anything we can imagine.